LATIN THOUGHT
DURING THE
MIDDLE AGES

The Roman Aqueduct at Segovia

See page vi

LATIN THOUGHT
DURING THE
MIDDLE AGES

BY

CESARE FOLIGNO

OXFORD

AT THE CLARENDON PRESS

1929

OXFORD UNIVERSITY PRESS
AMEN HOUSE, E.C. 4
LONDON EDINBURGH GLASGOW
LEIPZIG NEW YORK TORONTO
MELBOURNE CAPETOWN BOMBAY
CALCUTTA MADRAS SHANGHAI
HUMPHREY MILFORD
PUBLISHER TO THE
UNIVERSITY

Printed in Great Britain

CONTENTS

ERRATA

Page 15, *the quotation from Horace should read*:
Aetas parentum peior avis tulit
nos nequiores, mox daturos
progeniem vitiosiorem.
80, line 16, *for* Willibord *read* Willibrord
82, line 9 from bottom, *for* contibuted *read*
contributed
114, line 2, for *Liturgia historica* read
Liturgica historica
115, line 4, *for* 1911–24 *read* 1911–23
115, lines 9 and 8 from bottom, *for* 1909,
1921 *read* 1909–20
115, line 4 from bottom, *for* P. V. Winterfeld
read P. v. Winterfeld
120, *for* Willibord *read* Willibrord

Foligno: Latin Thought during the Middle Ages, facing p. v.

LIST OF ILLUSTRATIONS

LIST OF ILLUSTRATIONS

The history of this famous MS. provides evidence of the part played by different races in keeping alive the tradition of learning and of Latin scholarship. The text, of eastern origin, was arranged and penned at Capua, in southern Italy, about the year 546, in uncial (Beneventan) script. It was twice read by Victor, Bishop of Capua, whose hand is recognizable in the word *sumptum* written in the right-hand margin of the illustration. It has been suggested that this MS., as well as others perhaps, was brought over from Italy by Theodore, Archbishop of Canterbury, in whose following was Hadrian, the abbot of a Neapolitan monastery. The marginal notes are penned in an old Irish hand, according to Traube, and though there is no evidence that any of them are written by Boniface, an Anglo-Saxon, it is confidently asserted that the MS. was used by Boniface and was taken by him to Fulda where it still is. There is even a tragic particular in this story, for it is said that when Boniface was attacked and slain by heathens (754) he tried to shield himself with a MS. of the Gospels, and the original boards in which the MS. is bound show a deep cut that may well be the mark of a sword thrust. The author is indebted to Dr. E. A. Lowe for this photograph, which was taken by the kind permission of the Director of the Landesbibliothek of Fulda.

The fresco is cut out and framed with the inscription 'Caroli M. Imp. Effigies nongentos ante annos tectorio depicta S.S. Benedicto XIV P.M. a Clericis Regularibus devotis Nomini Maiestatique Eius oblata.' It appears therefore that the painting which is supposed to have existed on the Pincio was presented to Pope Benedict XIV (1740–58); its date cannot, however, be earlier than the late fourteenth century. Thus the place of origin, rather than the date and reliability of the picture, is significant, Charlemagne having received the imperial crown in Rome and having been the first of the Germanic sovereigns to be recognized as Roman Emperor. With him was initiated the *translatio imperii*, and around him took place a brief revival of studies brought about by the collaboration of Irish, Anglo-Saxon, German, French, and Italian scholars in a land where the traces of the Latin tradition were still perceptible. The fresco is reproduced by kind permission of the Director of the Vatican Galleries who had the painting specially photographed.

THE EMPEROR JUSTINIAN, from the mosaics in the church of St. Vitale at Ravenna (built before 547)   *Facing page* 106.

The emperor has on his left the Archbishop Maximianus and clergy, and on his right court dignitaries of whom the first may be Belisarius.

It was due to Justinian's initiative that a collection of Roman laws was made which was intended to remove all uncertainties of interpretation for all time, and which provided, on the contrary, the basis on which medieval lawyers built up a new jurisprudence as soon as conditions allowed for a revival of legal studies. *Photograph by Anderson.*

I

ROME AND THE MIDDLE AGES

IT is as easy to take the Middle Ages as the background of legends and fantastic stories as it seems to be difficult correctly to appraise that epoch in its complex reality. Just as there are nations and individuals who seem never to succeed in living down certain opinions about themselves which may or may not have had some justification at one time but have long ceased to have any basis in fact, so the Middle Ages have often suffered through the after-effects of old misunderstandings. The Renaissance dawned when the Middle Ages were setting: and the men of the Renaissance saw merely a period of decadence which followed upon the downfall of the Western Empire. Medieval learning and art could scarcely have any claim to the attention of Renaissance scholars who judged everything by the standard of ancient Rome and ancient Greece. There arose later a reaction against classical standards and against classicism; and the men who promoted this reaction were more favourably disposed towards the Middle Ages, as representing a direct opposition to classicism; they admired the Middle Ages because, in the course of the centuries so described, the ancient world was supposed to have been destroyed by the advent of Christianity and the barbaric invasions of Western Europe. Their admiration was thus based on the negative rather than the positive activities of medieval men. It was only later realized that the Middle Ages had created besides destroying. Allegories, romances, epic cycles, Gothic architecture were clear evidence of a positive contribution; but the source and the successive stages of this contribution were inadequately known, and, where historical accounts would have proved scrappy and unsatisfying, traditions gained credence and became established that were closer to legendary fictions than to historical truth. It was as easy as it was convenient to dissemble lack of information and inadequate investigation by prefacing any work dealing with medieval events with platitudinous remarks about the 'dark' ages, an epoch of senseless strife, of internecine feuds, of migrating peoples who seemed to have flitted from country to country without any plan or object unless the object of destroying the ancient world—its buildings, institutions, and civilization—so as to render more conspicuously heroic the exploits by which modern men succeeded in restoring civilization and restoring order out of chaos.

Tacitus himself started this fashion by the manner in which he described the conditions prevailing across the Rhine in his days: forests, hordes of flaxen-haired savages, wars and primitive customs. And, later, the inborn craving for romance made it pleasant to assume that medieval epics merely echoed the collective voices of peoples living under chaotic conditions and that legends were not the outcome of imaginative and artistic elaboration but the true representation of fact. For generations now scholars have laboured at elucidating every section of medieval history. Despite this the adjectives which more commonly are applied to the Middle Ages are 'dim', 'dark', 'little known', as if the idea of something misty, confused, wild, and mysterious was inseparable from the period which followed upon the fall of the Western Empire. Macpherson is almost forgotten, but the 'Ossianic' conception of the Middle Ages seems more difficult to displace, although these generalizations are wholly unjustified. Such knowledge of the past as is commonly possessed is mainly based on books; and the authors of books must needs insist, when describing historical conditions, on that which was peculiar to each period, and precisely on the characteristics differentiating that period from other periods; just as they are wont on the other hand to overlook the vast amount of facts and conditions that, being inherent in human society, are common to all ages and peoples, and are left to the reader to surmise. It is easier, moreover, to feel the bond of common human nature when a tale of love or sorrow is told, than when the subject is a great social and political upheaval. Just as the sun shines with pitiless splendour on the most tragic events, life with its minute and prosaic necessities runs on, even when sorrow befalls a family or a revolution seems to shake the very foundations of society.

As compared to the order and discipline of the best days of the Roman rule, the Middle Ages were troubled and agitated, no doubt. The rhythm of social and political development was jerky; security was impaired; the tenure of land and the possession of capital, when capital existed, were insecure, educational facilities were sorely diminished, and the delicate machinery of external and internal trade ceased to work smoothly. But the sun shone, the winds blew, the seasons succeeded one another, men were born, grew, worked, and died. They ate, slept, cooked their meals, if more simply; they read and wrote, if less profusely; they bought, sold, and bartered their goods; they even pleaded their cases in law; in short they lived. This is a platitude of course, but one must sometimes insist on platitudes lest the search after originality and concision make one lose the sense of proportion and the touch with reality. Moreover, of the two elements—continuity and change—during the Middle Ages continuity was traceable to Latin thought, and change to the new peoples that were settling in Western Europe. In a sense, the history of the Middle Ages is the history of the manner in which the old world reacted to Christianity, and the new races reacted to the old world.

Before she fell Rome had become Christian, and Christianity had acquired many Roman peculiarities. The history of the Middle Ages is also the history of how Rome conquered the barbarians through the Church, and conversely how the barbarians came under the searchlight of history, first by getting into touch with, and later by accepting Christianity from, Rome. Civilization and progress may be measured during the Middle Ages by the extent and importance of the Latin survival; for the Middle Ages start from Rome, from the political downfall of Rome, and end with the Renaissance, which is called a revival of classical ideals but would be better described as the discovery that on the whole the Middle Ages had caused a regression. Great changes had occurred, while some eight or nine centuries went by; but at the end, as at the beginning, the world was inspired by Latin conceptions, and it had been guided throughout those centuries by Rome, by Roman ideas and Roman traditions. Rome was no longer the centre of political power, but she had become the centre of Christianity, and she had always remained the centre of the world, the starting-point and the ideal of the medieval world.

There was something massive and crushing in Roman civilization, a forcefulness the very thought of which tends to awaken instinctive antagonism and to lack all power of aesthetic attraction. It was a miracle of adaptation, organization, and assertiveness almost irritating in its efficiency, as it was distressing at other times in its lack of elasticity. The student is often repelled by, and is unwittingly inclined to lay stress on, such portions and aspects of the massive structure as allow its flaws and its cracks to be perceived. But one must guard against so obvious a temptation, precisely because so many have yielded to it to a greater or a lesser extent. As usual there is pleasure to be got out of yielding, and it is tempting to show how much of what is called Roman had been borrowed by the Romans from the Etruscans, the peoples of the East, and the Greeks; to show in how many departments, in speculation, art, and literature, the Romans fell short of their models; to trace in writers and political men of a later imperial period the signs of an imperfect assimilation by Rome, signs of Ibericism, Gallicism, Africanism, and Hellenism. Once again the attraction of that which is rare, choice, abnormal, and the repulsion provoked by the massive uniformity of Latinity, must be resisted; once more it is the obvious which matters. And it must be faced in its crudity. A small agricultural stock in the course of three or four centuries established its supremacy in Italy and in the Mediterranean by force of arms and the power of discipline; it boasted no artistic gifts, it possessed no great originality of thought; it rather despised, on the contrary, the refinement of art

5

and the niceties of speculation. The source of its strength was to be found in social discipline, military valour, and common sense. So much so that it accepted foreign religious symbols and creeds with facility, it imported gods as well as philosophical theories, and these it adapted to its requirements with undiscerning eclecticism; it imitated foreign art without the slightest compunction, just as if all these things, which one is inclined to consider the essential manifestations of the mind of a race, were of no great importance. And in a way they were of little importance to the Romans. 'Graecia victa ferum victorem cepit' is a pessimistic dictum expressing only part of the truth. One could show that Roman life by degrees was profoundly modified owing to these accessions, that the very strength and power of Rome were sapped as a direct and indirect consequence of such an indifference. But this would imply a greater concern with what might have been than with actual events. It would be a manifestation of that strange, if common, tendency to escape from reality that causes us to talk of the disease that has caused a great man's death as of something that should have been averted, and to concentrate our attention on the tragedy of this death and on the things he might have done if he had not fallen ill and death had spared him; and what really matters, the record of his achievements, his life and his struggles, is almost forgotten. The most striking trait of the Romans' character admittedly was common sense; it is surely right then in their case, if not in all cases, to deal with their achievements from the angle of the plain man of common sense. From such an angle it is readily seen that for centuries the Romans, inartistic, unphilosophic as they were, not only conquered a large part of the known world and absorbed the arts, creeds, and theories of their more civilized and refined subjects, but rapidly enlisted the help of these subjects and turned them into agents of Roman civilization, just as so many of the young men of the conquered armies were turned into slaves.

The defects of the Roman organization are easily perceived, but the Romans succeeded in impressing a mark upon the ancient world which cannot be effaced. They did not strive for uniformity, and did not attempt, for instance, to suppress the Greek language, but by the time when their power was on the wane Latin was taught throughout the West and understood in the East; authors of Greek speech and education chose Latin as their medium of artistic expression. Wherever the Romans reached, they brought with them that syncretic complex that is known as Roman civilization: camps, colonies, forts, roads, schools, Roman law, and the Latin language, for the conquered barbarians lost even their languages. Such an achievement can only be paralleled by the United States of America, for the great Federation, if under widely different conditions, is also able readily to absorb and rapidly to assimilate foreign elements, ethnic, social, and cultural; turning settlers into loyal citizens as quickly as they learn the national language.

During the fifth century of our era the last remains of Rome's political power were wiped away. Though the Empire had long been shaken by the clash of disruptive forces, it may be said that as a result of the fall of Rome order of a kind was succeeded by chaos; an orgy of destruction followed upon an era of construction; the oneness of the Roman Empire was split into the variety of its component parts; hordes of barbarians as yet untouched by Roman civilization swept over all parts of Europe; barbaric tribes that had acquired influence by bolstering up weak emperors posed as the heirs of imperial authority; there seemed no hope left and no rest. Rome appeared to be dead and destroyed. But when the first centuries of the Middle Ages were over it was found that everywhere and in all departments of social life and culture Rome had survived. So much so that the peoples of Italy, Spain, Portugal, France, and Rumania, besides other minor groups, spoke languages which directly derived from Latin; that the whole of Europe followed a faith which had been reluctantly accepted by Imperial Rome, whose official language was Latin, and whose organization and tendency to universality had been inspired by Rome. It was found that the only language of learning was Latin, that the immediate sources of whatever knowledge had come down from the ancient ages were Latin, that whenever there was a period of intellectual or political revival the leaders consciously or unconsciously endeavoured to conform to Roman traditions; that art and literature went back for inspiration to Roman art, or to Greek art as accepted and transformed by the Romans; in fact that the immediate basis of medieval culture was Latin. It could even be said that the basis of modern culture is Latin, but that would be another story.

In the north of Britain there is a straight wall which centuries of struggles and the agency of time have not destroyed; in the deserts of North Africa enormous structures lie buried—cities, temples, canals, and forts— which the Romans have built; in Spain wide valleys are spanned by Roman aqueducts; in Rome herself one cannot move a step without being confronted (even now, after the wanton destruction of the Middle Ages, the senseless spoliations of the Renaissance, and the upheaval of the nineteenth century) with imposing remains of ancient Rome.

These are no more than symbols; their real importance is symbolic. It used to be said, 'Scratch a Russian and you will find a Cossack'. How true such a dictum may be, we would leave others to decide, but it would certainly be true to say, 'Scratch a cultured man of the Middle Ages and you will find him a Roman at heart'; for in every cultured man of that epoch, deep down or on the surface, clearly marked or dissembled, there is to be traced the Roman impress, and it will be our object to show how and why this came about.

II

THE SALVAGE

By degrees the structure of the Roman Empire became unwieldy, and some Romans began to note ominous signs of decay. The rural classes lost contact with the civilized cities, and turned against them. Christianity postulated the equality of all men, and Roman economy was based on servile labour. The defence of the boundaries under the later emperors was more willingly entrusted to barbarian mercenaries than to the citizens: isolated barbarians at first, and later, tribes or associated tribes of barbarians. The corruption and greed of the central government; the tyranny of the military element; the removal of the capital from Rome to Milan and to Constantinople, were contributory causes of the downfall. The organism of the Empire became increasingly weak; and the pressure on the frontiers, despite prudent retreats, became irresistible. The more intelligent among the barbarians grew aware of their power, and, according to their circumstances and individual inclinations, sought personal advantage either by standing up as champions of the Empire or by profiting from its weakness. In either case they had their own interests in view. But Rome in the end cast her spell on them, whether they confronted her as defenders or foes. Stilicho fighting for the Empire against Huns and Vandals became the most powerful man in the state, a sort of national hero whom Claudian, an Egyptian, belauded in his Latin poems as the champion of Rome. On the other hand, Attila led a reckless medley of ferocious barbarians in an almost successful attempt to destroy the Empire by the unrelenting blows of a military sledge-hammer. But Attila was at last driven back by the Roman Pope, Leo I.

Again, these are symbols. The importance of Attila's activities in western Europe is to be measured by the harm he was able to inflict upon the Roman world; it is as if he came under the searchlight of history only when he was hurling himself against Rome, and the most impressive scene was enacted on the Mincio, where 'God's scourge' unexpectedly withdrew at the bidding of Leo I, when the road to Rome lay open before him (451). The papal success was so unhoped for that it was ascribed to a divine intervention: angels with flaming swords were supposed to have frightened the superstitious barbarian, who was perhaps merely overawed by the presence of this saintly representative of the Roman world and by the very magnitude of the crime he was about to commit.

The Church acquired much political prestige through this bloodless victory; for the Western Empire was not yet officially dead when the Church of the West stood forth as the natural protector of Roman civilization. Let us take another example. Theoderic the Goth marched from the East towards Italy with the leave, and as a kind of representative, of the Eastern Emperor, when the Western Empire had already fallen. He ruled with a fair amount of success over Italy, but he never ceased to hold and describe himself as an imperial official, for he still belonged to that class of barbarians who were so impressed with the majesty of Rome as to aspire to no greater honour than that of defending the Roman Empire. He was almost the last of this kind, for the unreality of the Roman power was soon to become apparent. The political power of Rome was by then a fiction that could no longer be kept up; and when it ceased to restrain the barbarians there began a period of rapid decay and incessant destruction.

Meanwhile other invaders in other districts had swept over the borders and settled in every corner of the Western Empire; the process of settling implied the establishment of new states which were *de facto* independent. The period of migration was over.

For a long time the invaders had wandered and plundered; they camped rather than settled; a force was driving them westward and southward, just as birds fly south when winter is approaching, out of the forests and pastures of central and northern Europe to the ploughed lands and the cities; but they had been so long on the march that they scarcely realized that they had reached their ultimate goal. They were as travellers who, landing after a long journey on stormy seas, still feel the land wavering under their feet. It had often happened before, that a tribe or a people had no sooner won their way into a desirable province than some other tribe or group of tribes had followed in its track, and driven onward the earlier invaders. Thus it took time before the running waters realized that they had become stagnant. Stabilization occurred when the pressure from the east ceased or when the sea cut off further advance. Then the first arrivals were at bay and fiercely turned against those who still pressed them in the rear. Never would generalization be more unjustified than if one imagined Europe as a uniform land at this epoch. Each country had ethnical, social, and political peculiarities which distinguished it from other countries and regions, but all had certain features in common, for everywhere in Western Europe the Roman organization had been broken up by invaders, and everywhere the original inhabitants remembered the past, and by that past the invaders felt irritated or awed.

It might be said that the cataclysm of her fall constituted a kind of consecration for Rome. Her influence grew when her power ceased to exist. Rome fallen as a reality acquired the irresistible glamour of a dream. Dead as a political force, she seemed to be endowed with the compelling power of a myth.

The variety in the different provinces was principally caused by the varying clearness with which each province remembered the past and reacted to the myth, as well as by the different modes and effects of the awe with which the invaders or new settlers were struck. An adequate analysis of these differences would result in a historical examination of the social, political, and intellectual conditions of Britain, France, Germany, Spain, Italy, and North Africa: a stupendous conspectus which may well be attempted, but must be almost impossible to carry out satisfactorily. It should suffice to call forth to our imagination a picture deficient in detail but true in the main, and expressed in terms which are easily appreciated by the modern mind.

There are two difficulties, however, which must be overcome: the first arising from a mass of superficial notions which seem to lurk insidiously in the mind whenever the name of the Middle Ages is mentioned— text-book notions which had better be put aside from the outset; and national prejudice, the incidence of which is proof positive that the study of this epoch, far from being of a purely academic interest, touches modern men to the quick. For, modern nations having been formed during the early medieval era, it has been almost impossible to those who have written about this era to divest themselves of national preconceptions, with results that have sometimes been comic. The endeavour to eschew both these dangers may entail the restatement of well-known facts and lead to dullness, but it is an endeavour worth making.

During the days of the Roman Empire voices early arose pessimistically forecasting its downfall. Whilst some of the greatest buildings were being erected and the Roman legions still advanced on their conquering march or checked the enemies on the Rhine and the Danube, voices were raised to lament that the Roman ideals were being betrayed; there were men who perceived that wealth and luxury, Hellenism and sloth, necessarily would at first impair, and later destroy, Roman power. In the course of time the portents became so clear that the pessimistic utterances grew more numerous and distressful. Such a strange premonition of impending evil, to which the rising tide of Christianity probably added poignancy, was based on an implied premise: the existence of Rome was in itself to be considered a boon unparalleled and the necessary foundation of civilized society. The downfall of Rome meant the downfall of civilization. Thus the more conscious men grew of the dangers ahead, the greater became their insistence on the glory of Rome. A boon is never so clearly realized as when it is imperilled, just as awareness of the importance of good health increases when vitality is failing. It would of course be absurd to hold, as it would be impossible to prove, that the Romans became aware of their own greatness when they ceased to be great; it can be asserted, however, that their awareness grew then more explicit. The old pride in the Roman name and in Roman character by degrees gave way to the pride in Roman achievements and in Rome herself. The object which had been a spiritual force became a material fact; a driving force declined into a static sentiment, until it was reduced to the yearning torture of regret; and regret was naturally loudest in its expression.

Is it necessary to exemplify? Horace, who had sung the glories of Rome, proclaimed his pessimism:

> Aetas parentum prior avis tulit
> nos nequiores; mox daturos
> progeniem vitiosorem.

And Seneca (*Controversiae*, i, praef. 6–7) lamented:

'Since Cicero's days things have gone from bad to worse; partly because of our increasing luxury, for luxury is always fatal to genius, partly because there is no prize left for the noblest of the arts [oratory], and all our energies are given to the vices which now win honour and wealth; partly because nature's stern law requires that all high achievements shall end in a fall swifter than our ascent to the heights.'

Seneca had been born at Cordoba in Spain and may be reckoned as a fair sample of the majority of provincials who readily gave their full allegiance to Rome. If there was any resistance here and there, it was mainly stirred up by the ruthless exaction of taxes. In general the subjects of Rome identified themselves with the Romans and even carried the show of their loyalty to extremes: theirs was the snobbishness of middle-class people who have married into the aristocracy. Quintilian and Martial, Spaniards both, were almost irritating in their pose: Quintilian pretending not to understand a Spanish provincialism and Martial slightingly speaking of Bilbilis, the town whence he hailed.

Despite occasional outbursts of local patriotism the inhabitants of the whole empire felt themselves to be Roman; but the days of confident growth soon seemed to vanish; obstacles arose and heavy blows fell. Success did not prove satisfying; a stirring towards loftier ideals was quickened by the growing influence of Christianity. At first the signs were perceived by a few only; later the world seemed to rock on its foundations. What was this? Roman legions had been defeated before, but victory had at the end always smiled on the Roman eagles. Now it was in vain that the state called the sturdy barbarians into the army; in vain did it even seek the alliance with other tribal groups, and grant them land; in the past it had been Rome that went about looking for her foes, suppressing all the obstacles in her path. Now all the world seemed to be in a liquid state outside the boundaries of the empire. A mysterious process was going on; the enemies moved about, appeared from and disappeared into some strange waste beyond the lands on which the sun was shining. Tacitus had spoken of these new races beyond the Rhine. His very description invested them with the ominousness of mystery. And then they began deeply to penetrate into the provinces and even into Italy as ruthless conquerors. They camped in Rome herself.

Every child is familiar with some account of the downfall of Rome—text-books describe the terrible agony encompassed by the period between Alaric and Odoacer; but what one reads in text-books has a way of remaining cold and external. That tragedy will be a closed book for us unless we try, however feebly, to re-live it. Perhaps we are in a better position to catch something of its spirit than we should have been twenty years ago. There have been days during recent years when some among us felt that the cause of civilization was at stake. It certainly was at stake during the fourth and fifth centuries of our era. And it is that bleak feeling of despair that we must for a moment re-capture. That, and the disgust which was caused by the indifference and incomprehension of those who pre-ferred to shut their eyes to the impending danger, or who were too stupid to perceive it and lived in luxury and pleasure, danced and laughed and revelled when a crisis was upon the world. It seemed as if civilization went dancing to its death; and many a man, if he had known them, would have repeated the words which were said of Rome, 'moritur et ridet' (Salvianus, vii, 1).

When Alaric the Goth entered Rome (410) some-thing seemed to crumble: it was not a portent, it was a catastrophe. Rome had fallen. The world was at an end.

But it was not at an end. Precisely that ghastly impression of loss created a new Rome out of the ruins; in a sense it created two Romes. The legend of im-perial Rome had begun: while the city stood and ruled, it had enforced admiration and awe upon the world. But everything living reveals its limitations when it is measured by the standards of reality; the barbarians by their victories, the harassed provincials by becoming disaffected, had long ago revealed Rome's limitations; and the early Christians had despised heathen Rome. By ceasing to exist as a political force, Rome escaped from the standards of reality, and, however great and powerful in the past, she became greater and more powerful in the mind of early medieval men; greater for the barbarians who exploited her ancient domain, and greater also for those who called themselves Romans and naturally invested the past with the glamour of a Golden Age for which they were hopelessly yearning. In a sense Rome survived because she seemed to be surrounded by the halo of martyrdom and death.

It was a survival that implied a profound modification through the agency of many forces, of which provincial activity, Christianity, and scholarly instinct would appear to have been the most active.

One of the first effects of Roman decadence was the severance of the Roman from the Greek world. Roman thought, literature, and art had been fairly overmastered by Greek models and doctrines during the most flourishing period; but the assimilation was not still-born imitation. The results were no doubt less perfect if measured by the standard of artistic excellence, and yet the Latin adaptation did add something—a *quid* which is difficult to isolate, but which infused new vitality into Greek thought and rendered it, as transformed by the Romans, better able to survive during the troublous days which were to come. The Romans did not take everything that the Greeks had to give, but what they took they rendered more vital and lasting. They borrowed the columns from the Greek temples, but superimposed upon them arches and vaults instead of pediments and architraves. It could be argued that this process of adaptation was a creation *de novo*; and even acknowledging that in the process of adaptation much was deteriorated, it is still true that whatever reached the Middle Ages, and through the Middle Ages

the earlier Renaissance, from the ancients was transmitted through Rome and the Latin world. What
might have been if events had taken another course it
is idle to guess. Constantinople was in a far better
position to preserve the Greek legacy in its purity, but
her intervention scarcely exercised any influence. In
fact, it might be said with some justification that the
Italian Renaissance itself lost as much in vitality as
it gained in knowledge and purity when the scholars of
the West, in their restless zeal, secured the assistance
of Byzantine learning.

Thus the severance of the Western from the Eastern
world, by concentrating attention on Rome and on the
Latin world, accelerated and facilitated the process
by which ancient thought reached the Middle Ages.
Scholars who seem bent on drawing a continuous com-
parison between Greece and Rome to the disadvantage
of Rome have laid great stress on the Greek origin of
some among the best writers of the Roman decadence,
such as Claudian and Ammianus Marcellinus. The
Roman genius had become so barren, it is said, that if
a writer of any note did appear he was a Greek who
chose to write Latin. Quite so; the point is that they
did choose to write in Latin. Latin had become the
literary language of the whole of the Western Empire,
and it was strong enough to capture recruits even from
the East, where Greek pre-eminence was unchallenged.

In general the provinces had contributed much to
the glory of decadent Rome: Quintilian and Seneca
were Spaniards, a Spaniard was Martial, and Claudian
was an Egyptian. So much is made in our days of
the language test in questions of nationality that it is
strange that its significance in the Latin world should

so lightly be set aside. At any rate the imperial provinces played a considerable part in keeping alive the flame of ancient civilization and culture. Wherever and whenever conditions permitted, clear signs appeared that, despite all adverse influences—despite impoverishment, warfare, military despotism, rebellions, and invasions—the Latin culture survived.

Here, again, national prejudice has tended in modern days incessantly to obscure the issues. Much has been made by some scholars of stray bits of information which were taken as sufficient evidence of the cultural pre-eminence of this or that province of the empire and thus disparaging, explicitly or by implication, the culture of other provinces and particularly of Italy. Such a discussion seems idle unless in so far as it may help to encourage a minute investigation of every possible source. It really matters very little to know where and of what parentage each eminent man had his birth, so long as he fully believed himself to be a Roman and consciously strove for the glory of the Roman name. Soon, however, another feeling could be noticed, a feeling of allegiance to the province and to the race of origin. The old Gallia Transalpina and the Provincia had early absorbed Latin civilization, superimposing it on the Greek civilization in the district which previously had been in close connexion with the Greek Massilia. Gauls had been noted and praised for their eloquence, and their schools had become so flourishing and famous as to attract also students from Italy. Gallic eloquence and culture seem to have evinced certain racial characteristics. Massilia was a Greek colony, and a knowledge of Greek was usual in her territory well into the third century. But the Gallic country early experienced the full impact of the invasions, and the poet's faith in Rome's survival and ultimate victory is tragic in its poignancy, so soon was it to be contradicted by the events:

> Obruerint citius scelerata oblivia solem,
>> Quam tuus e nostro corde recedat honos.
>>> (Rutilius, *de red.* i. 53.)

It was Rutilius who pronounced the final justification of the Roman rule:

> Profuit injustis te dominante capi.
>> Dumque offers victis proprii consortia iuris,
>>> Urbem fecisti quod prius orbis erat.
>>>> (*Op. cit.*, i. 64.)

And the mere aspect of Roman Gaul seemed to testify to this. What had been, however prosperous and peaceful some French scholar may represent it, a land in a primitive stage of development when Caesar occupied it, had become, in the course of decades rather than centuries, one of the most progressive, intensely cultivated and cultured regions of the Empire. The Roman ruins of southern France are adequate evidence of the deep imprint that Rome stamped on the soil; several emperors were born in Gaul, just as in an earlier age it was from Gaul that the first teachers of Latin rhetoric had come to Rome.

The Roman settlers in Gaul had been comparatively few, but their influence, and the influence of Roman administration and law, were clearly great. It must have begun even before the Roman conquest, for Vercingetorix had Latin lettering on his coins; and it was so great until the end that the popular language which was to develop in France was principally based on Latin, despite a Celtic substratum and constant inroads and settlements of Germanic peoples. Language, culture, and also writing tell the same story. The Latin literature of the pre-Carlovingian period in France has the ease and the looseness of tradition. When the Empire fell, Latin soon ceased to be a spoken language in the proper sense of the word, but it was not felt to be foreign or dead; and the script with which documents and books were penned was based on the Roman cursive hand and half-uncial characters, precisely as in Italy.

Thus Gaul, overrun by Goths in the fifth century, and occupied by the Franks under the Merovingian dynasty, retained a great potentiality of cultural development; the occupants themselves being forced rapidly to attune themselves to standards which they were as unable, as they were unwilling, entirely to destroy. Felix Ennodius, a Gaul who became Bishop of Pavia (521), sang the praises of the Goth Theoderic; Venantius Fortunatus, an Italian, settled at Poitiers and befriended the unhappy queen of Chlotarius II. But of the ancient provinces France was not the only one to play a great part, and her own greatest moment was to come later. In the earlier period her function and her cultural fate were not dissimilar from Italy's, the two countries being in constant connexion.

Stranger was the fate of North Africa. The sands of the advancing desert have yielded and are still yielding so many and so important discoveries to our archaeologists that it is now easier than it was heretofore to realize how complete the Romanization of that province had been. It had, however, preserved a character of its own. Some modern scholars would wish to discount literary peculiarities which traditionally have been ascribed to African authors; they used to be taxed with 'tumor Africus', a florid style verging on obscurity, and it is now contended that this was a general phenomenon—a tendency to rhetorical flourish which became more apparent whenever real inspiration was running dry. But, apart from any other consideration, tradition has its weight: a name would scarcely have been invented to indicate a thing not existing. Claudian was born in Africa as well as Dracontius and Fulgentius, and it was Claudian who bewailed the decadence of his days:

> ei mihi, quo Latiae vires Urbisque potestas
> decidit, in qualem paulatim fluximus umbram.
>
> (*De bello Gild.* 44.)

Augustine also hailed from Africa; and this champion of Christianity played a great part in the preservation of ancient culture. But Africa's function was shortlived; most of her best men were attracted to Europe, and to avenge the vices which Salvian lamented the Vandal invasion befell that region. A brief period of twilight persisted during the Vandal domination, and then Latin thought was submerged on the southern coast of the Mediterranean.

More complex and lasting was the connexion of the Iberic peninsula with Latin culture. Its inhabitants had fiercely resisted Roman domination at first, and it would seem, by the course of later events, that they also retained a certain liking for independence, despite the jeers of Martial and Quintilian at their native places. The destiny of the country seemed to be completely identified with the destiny of the Roman Empire of which Lucan, another Spaniard, had sung the foundation; but later this country had suffered so severely at the hands of Roman tax-collectors that a change was desired, and in a sense the barbarian invasions were greeted with relief. The Vandals passed through the peninsula, and not even the sea could stop their 'Wanderlust', for they crossed the straits into North Africa; but the Visigoths stayed in the land and firmly implanted themselves there, and their rule had some of the good features which Theoderic's rule showed in Italy. They were conscious of their military superiority, anxious to be the undisputed rulers of the country, and at the same time they were (at least their leaders were) sincerely impressed with the benefits of civilization and not averse to playing the part of protectors of the arts. At the opening of the Middle Ages there was born in Spain in the person of Isidore one of the men who seem to have been conscious of standing on the threshold of a new age, and thus to have considerably influenced it. It was mainly due to the part played by Spain that the results of the recent activities of North Africans were preserved, and it was characteristic of the Spanish intellectual activity during the Visigothic period rather to assimilate and preserve than to produce and modify.

Preserving the cultural legacy of the past and adding to it are the two activities by which a period of civilization may be characterized. No civilization can rightly be assumed to be exclusively concerned with either of these two activities; but the proportions vary almost to infinity, and it is precisely this proportion that it is so important and so difficult to detect. Isidore's *Etymologiae* is in reality an encyclopaedia drawn from many different sources. He was the brother and the successor of Leander, Bishop of Seville, owing to whose pressure King Reccared had become a Christian, and he was in correspondence with Gregory the Great. In his library there were secular as well as sacred books, and he had inscribed over it these significant lines:

> Sunt hic plura sacra, sunt hic mundalia plura;
> ex his, si qua placent carmina, tolle, lege.
>
> . . . . . .
>
> Hic geminae radiant veneranda volumina legis,
> condita sunt pariter hic nova cum veteri.

These lines may be taken to describe Isidore's outlook as well as his library. He evidently felt that stimulus, peculiar to an age of decadence, to save from wreck the essential elements of a culture which in his opinion was doomed; and he looked upon the present, the past, and the future from a standpoint which was new. Martial had been at pains to disparage his birthplace; in the days of the schoolmen national feeling often was submerged by the universality of Christian culture; but Isidore began his history of the Goths with words which reveal an intense patriotic and racial pride. In an age which was to see the rise of modern nations this impersonal summarizer of the lore of the past seems to sound the bugle-call of Spanish patriotism; he wrote: 'Omnium terrarum quaequae sunt ab occiduo usque ad Indos'—and it must be noted that characteristically he puts the West first—'pulcherrima es, o sacra semperque felix principum gentiumque mater Spania.'

Isidore is principally known owing to his *Etymologiae*, for it was a useful store-room of knowledge, otherwise difficult of access, which was partly destined to be lost in its original form. And thus this work may be said to be a symbol of Spanish intellectual activity during the Romano-German period. No original additions of importance were made to literature, but a goodly section of Latin works was copied and stored away, and thus a certain number of works were saved which otherwise would have been lost to our age. They were preserved in manuscripts penned in a beautiful and rather archaic hand, some of which are now to be seen in Italian libraries after having migrated in the course of the early Middle Ages through Ireland, England, and France; and the range of such a migration may help as a symbol of Spain's intellectual influence. Spanish pre-eminence, however, was cut short and partly transformed by the Arab invasions. Isidore died in 636; in 711 the battle of Xeres de la Frontera decided the fate of the greater part of Spain. Only the kingdom of Asturias, centred round Oviedo, was to keep up a flicker of Christian civilization in the peninsula, until Charlemagne brought his conquering troops as far as the Ebro, and re-established an intellectual connexion between Spain and France which was to be fruitful and of long duration.

Thus in France, in North Africa, and in Spain parts of the Latin culture survived whenever circumstances allowed it. Like a great bush fire, culture could not entirely be suppressed by the trampling barbarians. From the first there were some among the Germanic invaders themselves who felt attracted to it; others withstood its attraction, but only for a time. In the struggle between a world which was civilized and latinized and barbarians who were just then coming out of the darkness of their native forests and the loose organization of a pastoral state, civilization was bound to conquer, whatever its losses; and civilization meant Latin and Rome. Victory depended no doubt in part on the efforts which were consciously made for the preservation of the past, but the principal force helping to victory was to be found in tradition. No librarians, directors of museums, or archaeologists could by themselves save a civilization. It is only tradition that can enliven learned efforts; and it is the constant incidence of the force of tradition which characterizes the intellectual history of the early medieval period, and renders the transmission of Latin thought during the Middle Ages so utterly different from the conscious efforts of the Italian scholars of the Renaissance and from the lifeless continuity of the Byzantine period.

Two incidental queries could be made here: how did the Greek civilization go under, and what part did Christianity and the Roman Church play in this struggle? These queries will be best answered in considering the fate of Latin culture in Italy; for there, in the immediate proximity of Rome, the forces of tradition had a better opportunity of making themselves felt.

III

THE CHRISTIAN CONTRIBUTION

THE Christian Fathers rank among the earliest prophets of evil who forecast a terrible fate impending upon the Roman Empire, and they were naturally inclined to consider its downfall a consequence of, and a just retribution for, the hostility which the Empire had shown towards the Christians. When the Roman rulers altered their policy, they altered it in the face of considerable opposition, and it was soon apparent that, if the Christians had little to fear from the lay powers, the Church had also little to hope from the state. Some of the disruptive forces of Roman society were akin, if not identical with, or allied, to the Christian community. Thus Jerome's cry 'Romanus orbis ruit' may have been the expression of regret or of grieved satisfaction, but the announcement is there, and it found ready response. For centuries the Romans had been accustomed to be at war with barbarians on distant frontiers; it had become the state's policy to enlist them and to transplant them into its territory; and in the early days most of these settlers had been assimilated. But a decreased power of assimilation was precisely one of the marks of the impending downfall, although those who witnessed the events, as is their wont, were slow in realizing the significance of the portents.

Thus Alaric's siege of Rome in 410 came as a terrific surprise; and Attila saw to it that the lesson should not be forgotten. When the end finally came, it came ingloriously, and historians have remarked upon the indifference with which the official end of the Empire was received. Such a remark seems scarcely to be justified. It may be as natural as it is convenient to consider the year 476 as a historic date; historians thrive on dates, particularly when they seem to conclude an era, and school children are expected to remember that Rome fell in 476; 'the Western Empire fell when Romulus Augustulus was deposed by Odoacer'. But it was not a sudden or an unexpected death; for after a prolonged agony it seemed to pass away in its sleep. Why should the men living at that time be particularly struck with what was little more than a legal formality? Diocletian had ceased to reside in Rome; Constantine officially had transported the capital on to the Bosporus (330); in 402 Alaric had swept over the eastern provinces; Radagisus had led his warriors as far as Tuscany and was only checked at Fiesole in 405; in 406 the whole of Gaul was overrun by barbarians. Stilicho was killed in 408, Rome fell to Alaric in 410. When the Goth Stilicho disappeared from the scene, Aetius alone, another barbarian, seemed to be able to withstand the hoards of the invaders; when he passed away, Italy ceased to be defended by armies, and Attila held his hand when the country lay open to him, because a pope successfully pleaded with him for its safety. According to ancient historians Rome had once been saved by the geese of the Capitol, and the legends which soon grew up around the meeting of Attila and Leo are evidence that also this second escape was considered miraculous; Rome's end was expected and thus was already discounted when it took place. Moreover, this end was not an end at all; for Leo I by standing forth as her protector and the guardian angels by unsheathing their flaming swords in her

29

defence, as the legend would have it, appeared to be the representatives of a new Rome as mighty as the ancient one, but endowed with a different power: Rome eternal whose temples were being transformed into churches. It is not by chance that Raphael, painting in the Vatican, chose that meeting on the Mincio between God's scourge and God's representative on earth as one of the landmarks in the history of the papacy.

After that, what did it matter that a shadowy emperor should be superseded? Rome's real power was no longer vested in him. That is how contemporaries must have felt who were not concerned with subtleties of constitutional history, and looked at reality. Jerome himself had said it: 'It is twenty years that Roman blood is flowing between Constantinople and the Julian Alps . . . ubique luctus, ubique et *plurima mortis imago*. Romanus orbis ruit et tamen cervix nostra erecta non flectitur' (Ep. lx). A pagan poet of the same age, a Gaul, refused to admit the reality of the downfall of Rome even after the deed of Alaric; and yet he too shifted his ground, emphasizing among all Roman feats the universal character of the empire:

> Urbem fecisti quod prius orbis erat;
> (Rutilius, *De red.* i. 66.)

as if he felt that, even should Rome politically perish, the stamp of universality that she had impressed upon the world would not be effaced; and Roman laws, he was sure, would survive eternal:

> Porrige victuras Romana in secula leges.
> (*Op. cit.* i. 133.)

Rutilius was evidently trying not to let the evidence of facts prey upon his mind; Salvian wrote an almost

The Meeting of Leo I and Attila, a fresco by Raphael in the Vatican

See page vi

ferocious indictment of the decadent Roman Empire. Its sins and crimes had rendered God's punishment inevitable, according to this priest of Marseilles, who could be passionately eloquent, and was fond of drawing lurid pictures of the 'sins of society' in his days, contrasting the unforgivable sinfulness of the Romans, which was unredeemed by any virtue, with the primitive sins of the rugged barbarians, who were hardy and daring and not incapable of moral improvement. 'Rome is perishing,' he seemed to say, 'why should she not? She deserves her fate.' It was Salvian who wrote those oft-quoted words: 'Quis captivitatem exspectans de circo cogitat? quis metuit mortem et ridet? Nos et in metu captivitatis ludimus, et positi in mortis timore ridemus. Sardonicis quodammodo herbis omnem Romanum populum putes esse saturatum. Moritur et ridet' (*De gubern. Dei*, vii. 1).

Odoacer had not as yet performed his constitutional reform, of scarcely greater import than a change of Cabinet nowadays, and it would seem that all thinking people foresaw that a catastrophe was imminent, that the old order of things was coming—nay, had come—to an end. If Rome had fallen, as Troy is reputed to have fallen, in the full glamour of power; if she had come down with a crash after a bitter fight, it would be reasonable to look for contemporary dirges. But as she slipped down by degrees, of which the last was the least conspicuous, it is sufficient to note that the inevitableness of the end had been realized by many who forecast and justified it; and those who made these forecasts, if still alive, may have refrained from gloating over their success at divination. The silent masses had no means of expressing their feelings, for it is only in modern days that the correspondence columns in newspapers have been opened to them. The masses were silent, but let no one infer from their silence a lack of realization. No doubt they may have failed to hear of or justly to evaluate the importance of the abdication of Romulus Augustulus; for them it is likely that the end of the old order of things coincided with the inroad into their own province of a particular host of barbarians. War-lust and ignorance caused these barbarians to destroy what they could not carry away and even to kill those whom they could not usefully exploit as slaves. Empty houses, looted cities, burning temples, abandoned fields were quite sufficient to impress upon the people the simple idea that 'Roman power was no longer what it had been'. Is it perhaps contended that during the Great War the inhabitants of occupied territory needed to read a war bulletin in order to realize their own condition and the loss of their property?

On the other hand, this silence about the evanescence of the Roman Empire in the West may be legitimately understood to mean that the people, more readily impressed by reality than by phantoms, were without a clear perception of Rome's end. Rome still existed for them; from within her walls a power was exercised which could and did claim to embrace the whole of mankind. Moreover, the Church in the fifth century was fully Latin; during the first and second centuries the language of the Church had mainly been Greek, and later, no doubt, Greek ideas continued to prevail, but the leadership passed to the Latin element, to the Romans Jerome, Ambrose, and Augustine. What this change may have entailed it is not our object to tell. Looking from the outside one might say that Christianity seized upon what was vital in the Roman world and used it as a means to strengthen its hold upon the West. The very claim to pre-eminence which was made by the Roman pastor, when viewed from a worldly angle, is a recognition of the supreme power which Rome had previously wielded in the field of politics. The initiative was still with Rome; when legions and officials were failing in their function, monks and priests began to spread all over Europe and revealed themselves as more and more dependent on the Roman organization. Christian Rome was stepping into the place of imperial Rome. Let the old symbol be recalled once more: Attila, whom Roman armies could not withstand, receded before the Roman pope. The Roman pope, *servus servorum Dei*, was to be styled *Pontifex*, the name by which the Romans had designated perhaps their earliest magistrate.

In such conditions it was natural that, far from losing her grip upon the imagination of men, Rome should exercise an increasing attraction. And Rome meant Roman thought and the Latin language, with all the consequences that this would imply.

It would appear that by the advent of the barbarians the Romans were made aware that a crisis was approaching; they refused, however, to consider this crisis as other than transient, and felt that civilization must be reconstructed on the basis of ancient achievements. Precisely the same tendency which caused the ancient wisdom to be summed up and simplified for the benefit of the people who might in the future not have access to the original works of the past, when the barbaric danger approached, and plunder and destruction were reasonably feared, caused precious vases and other golden ware, statues and treasures, to be concealed and buried—an instinctive practice, no doubt, which was actuated by sordid motives, and yet one which ultimately spoke of hope rather than despair. It was a hope that no one living at the time was to see realized, but which was realized in later ages, during less troublous days, when men endeavoured to reconquer what had been partially lost, to pass from medieval summaries and adaptations to the ancient originals and to unearth such remnants of ancient art as chance and human ingenuity had succeeded in preserving.

This later stage, however, which is identified with the Renaissance, was conscious of the purpose of its endeavour and was opening up a new era by running counter to the tendencies of the Middle Ages. For the Middle Ages accepted and transformed but never restored anything; such few attempts at restoration as one finds in that period were due to exceptional causes. Thus Theoderic praised Symmachus for his care in repairing the theatre of Marcellus; but Theoderic was flattering himself upon being within the Roman imperial tradition, and can scarcely be brought forward as an example of the medieval attitude to the classical past. Also the Church took over many heathen temples, but, far from attempting to preserve them in their original form, characteristically adapted them to the requirements of the new cult. In other circumstances and climes a new religion might have aimed at securing and marking its triumph by a wholesale destruction of ancient temples; but this was not the Roman way, and certainly it was not what Christians did.

In literature and philosophy the same tendency was evinced despite a considerable period of uncertainty and an all too human contradiction between intentions and results. The literary activity of the heathen days had been characterized in the later period by a minute labour of textual criticism, by a literary antiquarianism which indicated lack of creative power and a limited range of vision. The Latin Fathers of the Church would probably have liked to use a new language, if such had been available, in order to emphasize the chasm between the new and the ancient worlds; but they wrote in Latin, a language which they had learned from rhetoricians and grammarians and which they felt compelled, however unwillingly, to admire in the works of heathen authors. There arose thus a nice difficulty of divided allegiance, and it is well known how much the learned Jerome suffered through it. Jerome sums up in himself the conflict between heathen artistry and Christianity. When he withdrew to Jerusalem he took with him the classical library which he had carefully collected in Rome. Cicero comforted his fasting, Plautus allayed the horror called forth by the awareness of his own sins. In a sudden vision a supernatural voice reproached him: 'Ciceronianus es, non Christianus'—'Thou art a Ciceronian, not a Christian.'

The contradiction between heathen culture and Christianity was thus dramatically stated by one of the early Fathers; and the history of medieval thought could be described as the centuries-long attempt at reconciling the opposing terms of Jerome's dilemma. It was he too who forecast in his letters the main arguments on either side and the lines along which a solution was to be found. Even though he could make a vow to read no longer in his classics, he had no means to cancel from his mind what he had previously read. The classical tradition could be opposed, not denied. And after all, why should classical examples be eschewed in Christian works, if their evidence was telling? There are traits in the books of the Prophets which seem to depend on some classical source; there are passages in St. Paul's writings which clearly echo well-known classical lines. When Petrarch, at the close of the Middle Ages, wrote a letter in order to allay Boccaccio's religious scruples and to reconcile him to the study of the classics, the poet of Laura had recourse to the evidence provided by Jerome, and developed his argument with the coolness and sureness of an age in which such a conflict had become obsolete. But Jerome had none of this coolness; he suffered, prayed, and fasted in order to find a way out of his difficulty; in trouble and confusion he seemed to grope for it and to be unable to follow it in peace. The contrast between Jerome and Petrarch points to the passing of the age intervening between them, as their intimate connexion with each other shows the continuity of thought during that age.

Jerome, a true lover of poetry, suffered in sacrificing his profane learning to his belief, and his anguish found expression in words which were modelled on the style of the works he wished to renounce. A middle way was impracticable, a conciliation unfeasible: let no Christian learn anything of heathen lore; the same lips should not pronounce the name of Christ and that of Cicero. Ambrose and Augustine, whose intellects were less saturated with rhetoric, were less bitter and extreme in their pronouncements; but of course it was Jerome's 'extremism' which prevailed; it was by that extremism that Gregory the Great and Gregory of Tours were inspired.

Gregory's famous outburst against the idle limitations of grammar has mostly been taken as evidence of the decadence of Latin learning at Rome; it really proves, on the contrary, that he was conscious of his own grammatical disabilities and sensitive to possible strictures upon his own style. Would a man inveigh against the formality of table manners unless he were doubtful of his own and peevishly afraid of being criticized for a lack of social polish?

Gregory, however, is rightly quoted as evidence of the antagonism of the Church to heathen learning. At the end of the classical age this antagonism was more emphatic because of the persistence of the classical tradition. And this would seem to be conclusive proof that the ancient learning and creeds were not wiped off the face of the world at the beginning of the Middle Ages, if any proof were needed that so profound a change could only be slow. Those who think and write about human events, no matter whether ancient or modern, are confronted at every turn with the fallacy inherent in every true statement. Statements are made which clearly describe a real event or repeat a true judgement, such as 'Charlemagne was a successful ruler'. But such a statement was relative and not absolute in the author's mind—he did not mean to imply that every act of Charlemagne's proved successful; the reader on the contrary passively receives that statement and more often than not is inclined to give it an absolute value. In particular, no statement is in need of more careful qualification than those which concern the conversion of the Roman world and of the barbarians to Christianity. For beliefs and traditions die slowly; and therefore readers must help the historians by intelligent reading.

During the fifth century the leaders of the Christian world were busy in demonstrating the pre-eminence of Christianity and the sins and drawbacks of paganism. Orosius, Maximus of Turin, are examples in point; they had to fight a long battle, for the men living on the land more easily turned back to heathen worship. Ozanam points out that special Christian solemnities were established in order to supersede popular heathen festivities which had been celebrated at certain periods of the year, so as to outflank the resistance of tradition: Candlemas, for instance, took the place of the Lupercalia. This was probably the outcome of an instinctive tendency to compromise, and as such may have received the blessing of Jerome.

If the countryside was difficult to conquer because it was less easily accessible than the cities and consequently less readily penetrated by Christian ideas, there were in the cities other centres of resistance—the drama, including all histrionic performances, and the *ludi circenses*. For men will ever dislike interference with their traditional amusements, and it was impossible for a spiritual religion to countenance the performance of spectacles in which moral considerations played no part. The attitude of the Christian Church could only be one of uncompromising condemnation. But men want amusement and diversion perhaps more intensely when their lives are harassed. Continuous gloom is unbearable, and the ribald laughter and the coarse jokes of the mimes did not cease, during the centuries which were to come, to be heard in the city squares, if under altered conditions—thus provoking the unceasing attacks of ecclesiastical writers and preachers as well as the official condemnation of the ecclesiastical councils against the drama and 'gens histrionica'. The lower forms of dramatic art and entertainment have mostly escaped the notice of historians (words and jests which were not written down can scarcely be known to a later age); but if the necessary evidence were available it would most likely be seen that much that one would call heathen and classical was perpetuated in the drama and dramatic shows, and that the repeated indictments by the ecclesiastical authorities had other causes besides the coarseness and immorality of plots, authors, and actors.

The evidence of the arts—I mean plastic arts in particular—could also be relied upon to prove the continuity of tradition; for the representations and symbols of Christian ideas were not independent of heathen motives and emblems. This the least observant visitor to Rome must realize when seeing the floral decorations of Pompeian character in certain catacombs, the banquet scene in the tomb of the heathen Vibia on the Appian way, next to similar scenes in the catacombs; the crowding of disconnected biblical episodes on the sides of Christian sarcophagi, because the sculptors were accustomed to describe continuously the successive episodes of a single myth on Gentile tombs. S. Salvatore of Spoleto, with its Christian origin and classical outline, and its purely classical decorations into which Christian emblems are worked, is a more evident illustration. But why further insist? The words of Prudentius are explicit: at the end of the fourth century he complained of the continuity of Gentile superstitions; and it requires no stretch of the imagination to realize that Gentile superstitions could not alone survive from the ancient world—that their survival, on the contrary, must be taken as a symptom, and postulates a large continuance of habits, beliefs, customs, and traditions from the classical to the medieval period.

IV

SUMMARIES

THE Church then had to fight against a tradition of heathen beliefs among the uneducated and of snobbish attachment to ancient art and philosophy among the more cultured classes. The Church meant the body of the faithful, from the most ignorant and simple convert to the learned Bishops; so that, given the divers tendencies in the Church and the conditions in which the Church had to pursue such a struggle, there is no cause to wonder if the means which were adopted seem to us contradictory.

The mystic monk recoiled from the corruption of dramatic shows, was terrified by the very names of Plautus and Terence, and included the whole of literature—Virgil not less than Catullus—in the same condemnation; there was nothing good to be had from them, nothing worthy to be learned in literature at all, the Gospels and the lives of Saints sufficed for all religious as well as cultural requirements. 'Don't read, pray!' could have been their motto. 'Pray! Don't read, and therefore don't bother to master the grammar and style for which Cicero and Virgil are celebrated.'

But such an outlook was too narrow-minded to help in all the complexities of the great struggle. There have been upholders of extreme political views who in our own days have proclaimed their scorn and their hatred for learning and culture; but we have also seen that these same extremists have been forced to pursue an intensive propaganda in order to attract the children to their 'reformed' schools. This modern parallel should enable us better to understand the apparent illogicality of the Church. If religious zeal was enough to impress the ignorant, to inspire the faithful, and to convert the simple pagans, Christianity could not hope to fulfil the mission which Jesus entrusted to His followers, unless also the reluctant traditionalists, the learned men who read Aristotle and Plato, the eclectics and the Stoics of those days, were attracted into the fold. Among the Greek Fathers there had been men of great learning and eloquence—Origen, Gregory of Nazianzus, and Gregory of Nyssa; the three principal luminaries of the Latin Church—Ambrose, Augustine, and Jerome—had been learned and had availed themselves of their learning, both religious and secular, in their ecclesiastical activities. If the Christian clergy was to lead the world, it was necessary that young men should be trained in the subtleties of philosophy, that they should be protected against the evil influence of lay, and possibly heathen, teachers. Christian teachers of the young were needed, and Christian schools were established. Schools and teachers: how and what were they going to teach?

The Romans had scorned schools in the days of their growth; but, during the Empire, schools and the rhetoricians had flourished; Greeks and provincials had taught in Rome; famous schools and teachers had existed in the Western as well as in the Eastern Empire: elementary schools, in which the necessary minimum was taught, and higher schools, in which the refinements of rhetoric usually received more attention than the principles of philosophy.

In order successfully to compete with their lay antagonists, the Christian teachers were bound to borrow some of the books from those whom they meant to supersede. It was, moreover, impossible for them to develop at once an entirely original method, for there are bed-rock necessities which have to be accepted from experience.

If the boys had to write, they had better be taught to write according to the best models; and it was no fault of the teachers if the best masters of Latin style had been heathens. Those schools were original enough which cut loose from the pedantic tyranny of grammatical subtleties and textual criticism by which learning had lately been distinguished. How was it then to be avoided that some among the Christian teachers, and the more gifted among their pupils, should admire the style of their principal models and be impelled to read more deeply in such dangerous authors?

And further, there was the stimulus provided by the decadence of the state and by the barbaric invasions. Something was perishing. The feeling of an approaching end was on everybody, whether they despaired, whether they hoped against hope in a revival of political power of Rome, or bitterly accepted the awful suffering as a fitting punishment for moral decay and a necessary preparation for a better world. The same pope Gregory I, who affected indifference to grammar, wrote that wherever he looked he saw sorrow, that 'moans of distress reached his ears from everywhere. Cities were destroyed, castles demolished, fields abandoned, the land was turned into a desert' (*In Ez.* ii. 6). Long before, Marius Victor had lamented that the barbarian danger was impending upon everyone, that the fortified villas, built in solid marble to last out the ages, were no defence against the invaders.

One must endeavour to realize how much such a feeling of uncertainty must have affected those who, having lived in a learned environment, could scarcely conceive a world stripped of culture. Would the fragile threads of cultured life be spared by the barbarians under whose blows castles were crumbling and towns turned to waste? Culture must be saved, and men of learning acted as if they were aware that the mission of saving it was thrust upon them. It is astounding to see how this mission was fulfilled. No doubt much work that now seems intentional and directed to an object was merely perfunctory, habitual, and instinctive; but if ever a complex phenomenon was deserving of a poetical description, it is this; for it is difficult to restrain one's enthusiasm when one watches how countless little acts, obscure tendencies in great and in little men, conspired to one stupendous result. Given the conditions which prevailed in western Europe during the fifth and even earlier centuries and down to the ninth century, what is surprising is not that so much of ancient culture was lost, but that so much of it was saved.

In such circumstances it is best to look at this process in its complex entirety rather than in its thousand details; and it is important not to overlook the part played in it by the Church. It is well known that during the later centuries of the Roman Empire culture had become deadened: eloquence had given way to rhetoric, philosophy to grammatical studies, creative literature to textual criticism, lyrical and dramatic poetry to senseless tales of love and adventure. Our own is perhaps less entitled than other ages to look with contempt upon such tendencies. The sources of inspiration were running dry, and a materialistic culture, pseudo-scientific and pedantic in outlook, was unworthily replacing the great legacy of Athens and Rome.

Men such as the celebrated Macrobius and Servius may be taken to represent the philological period of later Roman scholarship, barren in its punctilious precision. Not unlike the Alexandrine masters working on the text of Homer, these scholars aimed at establishing the text and the interpretation of Latin classics for a generation of readers who were no longer familiar with the Augustan language and purely classical conceptions. They represent the crystallization of the classics. Commentaries and notes are no doubt a proof of interest, but they are also a clear indication that the author so commented is becoming an educational instrument, an affliction for many people and a solace for a decreasing number of readers, of readers at least whose appreciation is decreasingly intimate.

When culture passes from the hands of amateurs to those of professional teachers, an age of decadence, and therefore an age of so-called transition, has set in. What needs to be explained seldom possesses an immediate appeal. And it was during the fourth and fifth centuries, at the hand of professionals, that the canon of Latin authors was established and that much of what the Romans used to read became obsolete and was lost —completely lost for the Middle Ages and almost as completely for the following period.

The Church was at war with traditional culture and with learning, because learning and philosophy were heathen; the barbarians were either violently antagonistic to every form of civilization or unfit to master anything more than the external and simpler forms of ancient culture. On the other hand, Christianity had no means or intention of providing a new learning; a minimum of culture was necessary to the diffusion of the Christian doctrines and to the performance of the rites, and the barbarians, or at least the least savage amongst them, were anxious to confront the conquered Romans on equal terms as regarded the essentials of learning. Such generalizations are unavoidably sweeping and therefore inaccurate in detail, but they may be taken roughly to represent the conditions prevailing at the time.

Thus the three principal elements of Western society moved, independently of one another, towards the same goal; one and all needed a simplified form of culture. The Roman traditionalist element needed it because it obscurely felt that the world was moving away from the past, and it saw no possible safety but in a return to ancient standards and ideas; these ideas having become remote and difficult to the politically cowed and spiritually christianized population, it was necessary to simplify them.

In its turn the Christian Church wished and aspired to penetrate the masses; it was not a refinement of culture that was aimed at, but a minimum of learning cleansed of the most glaring errors of paganism. The barbarians, as newcomers in the field, were obviously in need of elementary text-books.

Who was to provide for such distinct and yet parallel requirements but the best among the representatives of ancient learning and the most progressive among the Christian teachers?

Boëthius and Cassiodorus well exemplify this move-ment. With them there became established the peculiar tendency of later Roman culture to reduce into set schemes the sum total of what the ancients knew and the men of the time could use. The old Varro, during the first century B.C., among his almost countless works had compiled an encyclopaedic book on the nine arts called *Disciplinarum libri novem*; so practical a classification of the 'liberal arts' was not forgotten or overlooked. Augustine reduced the arts to the number of seven (grammar, logic, rhetoric, geometry, arithmetic, astronomy or philosophy, and music), excluding medicine and architecture; and this classification was further elaborated to suit the taste of the incipient Middle Ages by Martianus Capella at the beginning of the fifth century. This African scholar happily caught the spirit of his and of the coming ages. A pedantic allegory fills the first two books, and of the seven following books one is dedicated to each of the liberal arts. Mercury, on Apollo's advice, marries Philology, who is raised to heavenly rank and is accompanied by the seven liberal arts as bridesmaids. There is a certain charm in the peculiar clumsiness of the allegory, for it is easy to perceive how sincere was Capella's worship of learning: the imitation of Varro's encyclopaedia and the mythological apparatus are a link with the past, the mere fact of the allegorical structure a foretaste of a tendency all too powerful during the coming age, and the dry and lifeless summary of the arts a model which medieval teachers were only too prone to imitate.

But there is also something pathetic in Capella's undeserved success. It is as if the work of a faddy country parson were to be singled out for a centuries-long fame. There is nothing in his work to justify its success. A sincere admiration for scholarship was shared by many in his days, though Capella struck upon the apparently felicitous idea of giving wings to his admiration and raising Philology to heavenly status. The pedant made use of a fashionable device, allegory: his was a thin-voiced enthusiasm, but enthusiasm it was, and perhaps it gained favour on account of its sincerity; and his also was the pedantry of a rather unimaginative teacher, thus unconsciously providing a nourishment singularly well suited to readers of the coming ages. In fact, it is as difficult to discover any solid merit in the *De Nuptiis* as it is easy to perceive how it obtained so great a vogue; for it is typical of its age and has faults which must have struck medieval readers as merits.

Compared with the popularity of the *De Nuptiis*, if the word 'popularity' be understood with some discretion, the echo aroused through the ages by Macrobius' commentary on the *Dream of Scipio*, however considerable and resonant, falls into insignificance; and only Boëthius and Cassiodorus, incomparably greater figures than he, can contend with Capella for the primacy. Boëthius and Cassiodorus—the former of ancient Roman lineage, the second probably belonging to a family newly risen to distinction—lived both at the court of Theoderic the Goth.

It was characteristic of this notable barbarian that he had descended into Italy as a representative of the Eastern emperor and wished it to be believed that his authority was legitimate and not depending only on force. He chose Ravenna, a Hellenic city, as his capital, and stood out as a protector of the ancient monuments, while he corresponded with barbarian rulers and affected towards them a tone of superiority.

Whatever the appearances and the pretexts, it must

have been clear to many that a new order of things was being established. In Gaul the Franks under Clovis had made their position secure, and the Goths under Theoderic were taking up in Italy an unchallenged pre-eminence. Cassiodorus Senator, the faithful servant of Theoderic, maintained that the Goths were far superior to the other barbarians and were more susceptible to culture; but a world dominated by barbarians, for the best of whom a great Roman could find no higher praise, must have caused men such as Boëthius and Cassiodorus great misgivings as to the continuity of ancient thought. Such a peril was rendered the more apparent by the rapid decay of the language of civilization.

There had been a time when in the Roman Empire no man of education was not conversant with Greek; all who needed it had therefore direct access to the main sources of ancient thought. But, in the West, Greek rapidly receded from its former position with the advance of the barbarians or rather with the political decadence and the intellectual stagnation which rendered the barbaric invasions possible. Country folk who rose to power from the ranks of the army, soldiers of foreign extraction, the whole mass of new-comers who hurled themselves on the rich population of the cities, had no need of being familiar with Greek. One understands, then, how Boëthius was prompted to come to the assistance of his contemporaries and followers by interpreting for them such of the ancient works as seemed to him more significant. It would be absurd to suppose that Boëthius, who started his labours while still young, had either a clear plan or a vision of the requirements of future ages; but it would be equally unintelligent to fancy that there is no relation between the direction in which Boëthius developed his studies and the intellectual and cultural crisis which was actual or impending. Everyone is familiar with the name of Boëthius, but to most it merely conveys the recollection of a famous book *De Philosophiae Consolatione*, which was written during the period of imprisonment preceding his death (524). Theoderic is blamed for having inflicted an undeserved punishment upon so great a man, and is even supposed to have died two years later rent by remorse. It is practically impossible to judge how far the prosecution against Boëthius was justified; but whether innocent or guilty, his name and his work survived, and many generations of men during and after the Middle Ages read a treatise in which some of what is finest in ancient philosophy is distilled. His name seems to be surrounded by the halo of martyrdom, as if he had died, as ancient Romans had done, for the cause of justice. Despite this it would be no exaggeration to say that Boëthius's importance far exceeds the vast echo which his death and his last treatise aroused, for it was Boëthius who interpreted and translated most of such books of Aristotle's as were ultimately known to the Middle Ages, including the First and Second *Analytics*, the *Sophistici Elenchi*, and together with them Porphyry's *Introduction* to the *Categories*.

Some of his translations were provided with diffuse commentaries, and he also annotated philosophical works by Cicero and composed original treatises on arithmetic, geometry, and music. The originality of these works is to be evaluated according to medieval standards. It was the science of the ancients which Boëthius was handing down, and his work of trans-

The Tomb of Theoderic the Great at Ravenna

See page vi

mission was so effective that, before the age of the translations from the Arabic, little was known of mathematics but what Boëthius interpreted; and that, even centuries later, Gerbert, who has been hailed as the restorer of musical knowledge, was mainly indebted to the works of the philosopher who suffered in the tower of Pavia.

Directly or indirectly all his sources were Greek, but his treatment of them was Roman, with a tendency to the practical, and a certain unwillingness to discuss and decide subtle points. It has even been asserted (by H. F. Stewart and Dr. Sandys) that the great quarrel of the Universals—about the real and separate existence of *genera* and *species*—primarily depended on a point which Boëthius mentioned, but left undecided.

Despite the fact that Boëthius seems to have taken some interest in certain questions of Christian theology, there are scarcely any traces of Christian belief in the whole bulk of his philosophical works. He was a be-lated voice of ancient Rome explaining ancient theories and culture to an age which was, or seemed to him to be, in danger of becoming estranged from ancient wisdom.

Cassiodorus represented another link in the chain, a link which had no less importance, but a different function. A faithful civil servant for long years, an orator of considerable renown, a letter-writer with a peculiar sense of humour, a historian who sincerely or advisedly admired the dominating race, but a man who before the year 540, at an age between 50 and 60, on the eve of the Byzantine victory over the Ostrogoths, withdrew from public service and settled near Squillace, where he founded two monasteries, one of which, Vivarium, was to become famous. If ever there was an

instrument of fate, it was Cassiodorus. There is scarcely anything that is Roman in this worthy official. He seems to have been bent upon recapturing something which his age had lost and Boëthius was trying to transmit. Boëthius, a man of learning and culture, endeavoured to preserve the principal philosophical and scientific ideas of the past. Cassiodorus obeyed the summarizing instinct which was developing at that time when he composed his *Institutiones*, but that work had a practical object in view and his principal activity was practical. It was Cassiodorus who collected manuscripts, not only from Italy but also from northern Africa, for his monks; it was he, above all, who directed his monks to read and copy manuscripts—to copy them and to bind them. 'It is a happy thought', he wrote, 'and a praiseworthy occupation to preach with one's hands, to disclose lips with one's fingers, silently to bring salvation to mankind and to fight against the devil's illicit temptations with pen and ink.'

One understands how in such a spirit the weary process of transcription must have assumed the sacredness of a mission; the *librarii* were so called, according to Cassiodorus, because they *libere* (freely) served justice and God. A noble thought concealed in a miserable pun—a noble thought on which there follows immediately a happy pedantry. No manuscript could be of service to justice and God if, by mistaking one letter for another, the writers mixed wrong with right words or were unable through inexperience to emend a faulty passage in their original. Scribes who were, or thought themselves, learned enough to correct their originals have no doubt given more trouble to modern scholars than their less erudite or presumptuous fellows, but to

Cassiodorus great credit is due for having set so high a standard. Greater credit still he deserves for having directed the activities of his monks to the transcription of classical as well as religious manuscripts. The effect of his intervention was of first-rate importance in the history of culture; for the works which have reached us by any other route than monastic transcription are so few as not to deserve a special notice. One might say, indeed, that there is nothing extant of ancient literature, taking this word in its widest acceptation, that has not been copied and preserved for us by monks.

The manuscripts of an earlier date than the sixth century are exceedingly few; and Cassiodorus, though it is probable that the followers of Martin of Tours and of Benedict of Nursia had or would have started independently on so useful a path, may without injustice be hailed as the hero of this movement. Later, the Benedictines in particular, but also most of the other orders of monks, persevered in this work, and thus copies of ancient manuscripts were multiplied.

Of which ancient manuscripts, however?

V
THE SCOTTISH AGE

At the end of the fifth century there still stood countless monuments which crumbled during the later Middle Ages and the Renaissance, and there still existed manuscripts of works which are now irretrievably lost. The monuments perished through depredation, arson, and age; the manuscripts by degrees disappeared through disuse, when attention ceased to be directed to the works they contained. Libraries were looted and manuscripts burnt when cities were sacked and country villas destroyed. No less than in the case of institutions and traditions, in literature and art the Roman heritage was doomed, so long as it remained in the open, unprotected by the Church; only such works as found hospitality on the shelves of monastic libraries stood a chance of surviving the earlier Middle Ages. Thus the greater losses occurred precisely at the beginning of the intermediate age when the leadership of the Latin world was passing from the laity to the clergy, and the clergy was still imperfectly organized. It is not maintained that everything that the monks copied during the sixth century was *ipso facto* saved from destruction, but it may be asserted that a greater chance of survival was granted to it, and that, failing such a chance, oblivion was almost certain. How then was the choice made and what criteria presided at it?

Purely religious works are obviously outside the scope of the present survey, and classical works fell into several categories. There were masterpieces whose texts had been recently studied and established and which constituted models set up by the leading scholars for imitation. The grammarians and rhetoricians of the later Roman age from Quintilian to Priscian had naturally sought their examples in the works of Virgil and Cicero, to mention only two among the most famous names. Thus repeated mention in grammatical treatises, some of which were indispensable school-books, called the attention even of men of little culture and taste to Cicero's and Virgil's works. To a lesser extent Ovid and Livy, Sallust and Seneca, Juvenal and Statius, Tacitus and Tibullus, shared the same privilege. As a rule, little credit is awarded to grammarians; but let us give them their due and remember that, however unwittingly, they have contributed their share in ensuring the admission to the ark of salvation of a number of Latin works.

But grammarians were not alone in this particular contribution. It has already been seen on what grounds men such as Jerome and Augustine occasionally defended classical books against the sweeping condemnation of Christian mysticism: there was some good, they maintained, even among heathens. Some of their doctrines seemed reconcilable with Christianity, as if the leading spirits of the classical world had been granted an unconscious prescience of Christian truth. Everything depended on a correct interpretation of their meaning. In a world in which intellectual forces seemed to be straining towards the beyond, and to refute the positive realism which is peculiar to classical learning, it was easy to step from the literal to the symbolical interpretation. If the gods of Olympus were held by some of the Christian Fathers to be embodiments of angels and devils; if the books of the Old Testament were also held to be susceptible of another besides the literal interpretation, why should classical works be denied such a treatment? It was a process of unconscious conquest of heathen literature by Christianity, a process which was provoked perhaps in equal measure by the individual desire not to forgo the enjoyment of literary masterpieces and by the expansive strength of Christianity. To spread its power over the nations which had taken over the rule of the civilized world was not enough: missionaries went forth in all directions, towards the North and the East, in search of new races to conquer and to bring into the Christian fold, and like these missionaries there were zealous scholars, more noteworthy perhaps for religious fervour than subtle scholarship, who aimed at enriching the Christian world with the treasures of ancient literature.

The taste for allegory is sufficiently attested by the work of Marcianus Capella, but its beginnings go back to Origen for the Biblical books, to Athenian and Alexandrine critics of Homer, and, with regard to Virgil in particular, to Fulgentius.

The causes of the allegorical fashion are probably more complex than one would at first surmise. On one side there was the incidence of Christian ideas, for the intolerance of the zealots caused all works of the past to be considered works of perdition that did not allow of a more favourable interpretation than the ancients had known. Thus the masterpieces of Latin literature, precisely because their loss would have been instinctively felt as disastrous, were subjected to the efforts of the new interpreters. Allegorical interpretation seemed a master key to these early practitioners which would open any door. Virgil, for instance, was admired by Christians for his gentleness and purity so long as they preserved some literary taste, and these admirers, as well as other men who were impervious to the appeal of literary genius, were ready to attribute to him either a prescience or a complete possession of Christianity. The fourth *Eclogue* was taken as conclusive evidence on this point; and men of taste felt relieved in finding a Christian justification for their literary admiration, while others accepted Virgil as they accepted Prudentius and Claudian.

Virgil became the sage, the originator of Statius' conversion; his tomb was believed to have been visited by St. Paul. There were thus contributory reasons for the vogue of allegory, reasons which were connected with the evolution of literary taste.

Since the days of classical Greece two tendencies could be noted in prose-writers: a tendency preferring a direct and another favouring a more florid style. It would perhaps be more accurate to say that at all times authors instinctively tend towards one or the other of these styles. The florid style is generally in favour where luxury predominates, and external adornments are superimposed on, and more often substituted for, inspiration. Examples of such a tendency could also be found in our own age, for it is evident that, when the standard of literary perfection becomes uncertain and is sought in the works of earlier masters, skill in literary craftsmanship is more likely to be imitated than are the more solid qualities which go to the making of classical perfection.

There are many such tricks of craftsmanship, though

they may be grouped under a few headings, such as a peculiar resonance in prose rhythm, abundant imagery, and indirect expression. Thus, when an age is reached, or a social group is formed, in which literary taste is particularly debased, there may develop a liking for 'cleverness'—for dexterity in making remote allusions, for pregnant imagery, and, in fine, for obscurity. Such a taste finds then abundant expression both in new works and in the extreme subtlety by which remote interpretations are forced upon works whose authors were quite innocent of any symbolical intention. There have been orgies of obscurity among the writers of the later Roman period, such as the African Mamertus, and of the early Middle Ages when the *Hisperica famina* was composed.

A tendency to subtlety may thus be taken to have helped towards the fashion of allegory in writing and interpreting, which of course does not mean that allegories and allegorical interpretations need always be connected with it either in the fourth, in the tenth, or in the fourteenth century. These two aspects of the question were not of an equal significance, for the second of the two merely pointed to a debasement of literary taste such as in other departments of life would call gaudy colours and cheap adornments into fashion; on the contrary the former, as being an attempt at investing classical works with meanings and values appreciable by a later age, was just one of the most characteristic symptoms of the life of those days and may find a parallel in the turning of heathen temples to Christian use.

It is always easiest to seek for the expression of thought and sentiment merely in human speech and in literature, as if these were the only as well as the most immediate means of intellectual and sentimental expression. Such a temptation should, however, be resisted, for literature is but one of the manifestations of life, and its evidence may often need corroboration from other sources. It may be prudent to forgo such help as may be drawn from the arts—for they are at one and the same time too akin to literature in their development and, often, too dubious of interpretation—but it is necessary to pay attention to other fields of human activity.

For one, the technical means of literary expression—and by this I mean not so much style and grammar as handwriting itself, the medium which is employed to receive the impression of the quill, the manner in which the sheets of papyrus, vellum, or paper were put together and books were made up. Among the wider fields would be political history, and with it social and institutional history, the histories of law and rite—in fact the record of all the activities of the men whose thought we are attempting to follow. So extended a plan cannot be carried out in practice, but there may be occasions on which a departure from the beaten track will provide a useful check and offer an illuminating sidelight.

Quite apart from the elementary reflection that the mention and even the imitation of classical work is no evidence that such a work was fully understood, the degree of culture in a country or a province at a given date cannot be measured by the number of manuscripts which we still possess and which are known to have been penned or preserved in particular libraries, owing to purely accidental causes of loss or preservation. It happened for instance that, between the second and the fifth centuries, a technical revolution took place: the ancients were wont to pen their works on tablets and scrolls, but it increasingly became the custom at that period to use vellum instead, which could less easily be made up into a scroll. It is probably owing to this fact that so few of the earlier manuscripts have reached us; and, considering that in Italy the practice of writing on papyrus lasted probably longer (for we know of a work by Boëthius so written), we cannot infer that fewer manuscripts were written in Italy than elsewhere at that time merely on the ground that we find extant a smaller number of Italian than Spanish manuscripts of that period. The one legitimate conclusion to draw is that, even in the technical means of writing, tradition was strongest in the country which had been the centre of the empire; and it is a conclusion that one can ill afford to overlook.

It has also been noted that the practice of literal quotation was almost completely unfamiliar to the ancients and became quite common during the Middle Ages; this is, however, a change naturally consequent upon technical developments, for it is much easier to look for a passage when turning the leaves of a book than when one is forced to unwind a scroll. And again, there has generally been a parallelism between the intensity of literary activity and the neatness with which the words were written or impressed; thus in the Middle Ages the ebbing of culture could be followed in its ups and downs by the study of palaeography. There were schools and fashions in the script; and it has been shown that there have never existed national scripts differing from country to country, but one basic hand which was Roman and became variously modified according to the different standards of culture in the different places. Is this not precisely what happened to culture itself?

The hand which was used in Italy, in Gaul, in the Iberic peninsula, and in northern Africa showed certain possibilities of modification while keeping within the bounds of tradition, precisely because it was itself traditional. On the contrary, in the British Isles and here and there in France, it more rigidly kept to the older models because in those countries the force of tradition was weaker or missing.

At the end of the classical period the Latin hand was either uncial and half-uncial in books or cursive in legal documents. In course of time these two parallel scripts became confused, the half-uncial tending towards the ease of the cursive, the cursive aiming at the clearness of the half-uncial. The early English hand was based on the uncial, the Irish hand was shaped on the half-uncial; and it was in France that on the basis of the half-uncial, in the days of Charlemagne, a cursive script was developed which spread by degrees to Northern Italy, to England (ousting the Anglo-Saxon hand) in the eleventh century, to Spain, where no more Toledan manuscripts were penned after the twelfth century, and lastly to Southern Italy, where the Beneventan script was still practised as late as the thirteenth century. Verily one could read the history of Latin culture as in a mirror in the history of palaeography.

It was due to political reasons that the practical uniformity of later Roman culture became geographically differentiated. The political connexion between Europe and North Africa ceased, and Latin culture was extinguished in a blaze of glory when the Goth kingdom fell. Little was saved from that ruin, but the North Africans had by then contributed something to the continuity of civilization. And while there lasted in Spain the power of the Goths, it was given to the Spaniards successfully to labour both by transcribing texts written in Italy on to fine vellum penned in the Toledo hand, and by epitomizing learning as Isidore did. Spain seems to have had some connexion with Ireland, which had been converted to Christianity by Greek or French missionaries, and with Anglo-Saxon Britain, where Latin culture had been entirely suppressed by the invaders, and where it was reimported by the missionaries sent from Rome, one of whom at least was Greek, and even more by Irish monks.

Thus in Spain there was the continuity of tradition which was visible in the shape of letters, and tradition was on the contrary inexistent in Ireland and had been stamped out in Britain. What was the effect of this? That the Irish knew Greek as well as the Latin which they had learned from the Welsh missionaries of the second century (and they may have known Greek better than Latin); that they, as well as the Anglo-Saxons, had no vernacular basis for their Latin style and thus kept closer to classical models; and finally, as an outward mark of distinction, that they wrote a hand different in many particulars from the script which was prevailing in other parts of the old Empire.

Irishmen—who were called Scots—and Anglo-Saxons knew Greek, when Greek had been submerged in the older provinces of the Western Empire, but they possessed no local stores of traditional culture and of books on which to rely. They were thirsting for knowledge and most anxious to provide themselves with ever more numerous and choice manuscripts. The tendency and character of Irish and Anglo-Saxon culture differed as much as their scripts from the rest of western Europe. As races they had never been absorbed by the Roman Empire and romanized, they had had no share in the Latin civilization, the languages which they spoke owed nothing to Latin; but, from the moment in which they became converted to Christianity, they aimed at gaining possession of a culture which was to them the Christian culture. Their effort was primarily religious, and it was rendered possible by the work of the earlier scholars and saints who had assimilated ancient learning and recast it in the light of Christianity.

It was the second stage which was then beginning. During the first stage, by a process of attrition and re-elaboration, what was left of ancient culture had been attuned to the requirements of a composite population which was either entirely new to culture and civilization or less susceptible to them owing to the incidence of wars and depredations, despair and poverty. These characteristics of the second stage are more clearly outlined in the case of the Scots and Anglo-Saxons. The Scots were fired by religious zeal—learning with them was merely subsidiary to piety. In the seclusion of their islands they aroused in themselves Christian enthusiasm and a craving for martyrdom; they seemed to look upon the rest of Europe as a field in which to find scope for their restless activity. The biographer of St. Gall wrote that for them the habit of wandering had become a second nature, 'quibus consuetudo peregrinandi iam paene in naturam conversa est'. Their object was to widen out the boundaries of the Christian world and to deepen religious feeling where it appeared to them to lack the fire of asceticism and to be deadened by ignorance and corruption. The means which they adopted were preaching and the foundation of monastic houses of exemplary conduct.

But they had received learning together with Christianity, and learning had for them the added fascination of novelty. What learning had reached their island of origin was but a fraction of what the ancients had possessed, so that when they began to set foot upon the mainland, during the sixth century, they were amazed by the vastness of their ignorance; and with the same zeal with which they pursued Christianization and reform they also collected and transcribed, scouring the whole of western Europe, and principally Italy, Spain, and France, for ancient manuscripts written in the uncial and half-uncial characters which few were still able to read, in order to copy them in their scriptoria, to store them in their libraries, and occasionally to make use of the vellum by erasing the old writing. In so doing they were the direct and at times unintentional means by which a number of classical works were handed down to later periods and thus saved from destruction. As they were untrammelled by the use of vernaculars grounded on Latin and exemplifying a much altered form of the ancient language, they learned their Latin from books—perchance the Bible and perchance a classical or post-classical author—and they succeeded in acquiring a stylistic and linguistic polish which their contemporaries in latinized countries had mostly been unable to retain.

This rather unexpected consequence is even more readily noticeable among their Anglo-Saxon pupils— *scholares Scottorum* as they are called in an eighth-

A leaf of the Victor Codex of the New Testament of Fulda

See page vii

century manuscript—who were as zealous as their masters, but sterner, more sedate, and less inclined to wander. Scots and Scottish foundations are met with in Britain, France, Germany, and Italy almost everywhere. The Anglo-Saxons, on the other hand, began by consolidating their civilization at home, and only later followed the Scots on the Continent, where they were destined to fulfil a magnificent mission by becoming the inspirers of the Carlovingian reign and converting Germany to Christianity. Their activity was great from the time of their conversion: it was characteristic of them that, being brought face to face with what was to them a new world, coming into contact with a civilization which their forefathers had stamped out in Britain, they felt prompted to assimilate that civilization and learning by translating pious and famous books into their own language. But the Church had substituted a new and more efficient universality for the universality of ancient Rome—'urbs est facta quae prius orbis erat'—and Latin culture proved irresistible; the learned monks travelled to Italy in order to see Rome, the seat of the Church, came under the spell of Roman tradition, and went back to their country carrying with them manuscripts as well as relics. No doubt the indefatigable Scots, who were never tired of acquiring and transcribing manuscripts, helped them. But it was destined that the Anglo-Saxons should produce the most perfect stylist of the period in the Venerable Bede.

Shut up in his cell at Yarrow this pious and patriotic man well represented some among the best traits of Anglo-Saxon culture. History rather than speculation attracted him, the history especially of his own country since it had become Christian; prose he found a better medium than verse, and by ceaseless study he patiently fitted himself for his work. Some Greek he may have had, the Latin Fathers were familiar to him; but Benedict Biscop, his master, had taken back from his journeys to Rome considerable quantities of books, and among them classical books; and his master's example suggested to him a wide reading in the classics as well. Bede was no doubt unusually gifted, but despite his exceptional gifts he possessed many of the Anglo-Saxon characteristic traits and deserves special notice in consequence. Religious zeal was his real driving force; his liking for the classics was a mere matter of good taste. Of the several types of Latin which came under his observation, he preferred the best. His scholarly preference, however, did not entail either a whole-hearted worship of the ancients, such as was Petrarch's and his followers', or an admission of his own individual, and still less his racial and linguistic, inferiority. Good, plain, lucid Latin was an excellent medium in which to express his Christian feelings and the glories of the Church in his well-beloved land: he cared for his land and his monastery so much as never to feel prompted to leave them, and cared for his race and his language so much as to labour to his last days in translating the Gospel of St. John into Anglo-Saxon. This sturdy Anglo-Saxon became a good scholar and an excellent stylist, but he renounced nothing of what was his own, and never for a moment felt abashed by the greatness of Rome. In reading Augustine and Isidore alongside of Cicero and Virgil, he instinctively preferred the style of the ancients, and with truly medieval lack of historical perspective, being untrammelled by tradition, he felt no compunction in choosing his models according to his taste; thus acquiring a Latin style which may have none of the liveliness of the spoken usage, but which is perhaps the finest prose style that the earlier Middle Ages can display.

His contemporary Boniface became the founder of Fulda and the apostle of Germany, but the ultimate glory and the fulfilment of the mission of the Anglo-Saxons in the field of culture were due to Alcuin, whose activities had better be considered in connexion with the so-called Carlovingian Renaissance. It need only be added here that Alcuin also evinced several of the national traits so well illustrated by Bede. He moved, however, in a larger field, lived at court in France and travelled in Italy, thus coming into contact with traditional elements of culture which had had little effect upon Bede. There was still in Alcuin the Anglo-Saxon sturdiness, but he was not an isolated scholar, he was a man of affairs living at the very centre of the political life of his days.

VI

CHARLEMAGNE

No less than Charlemagne's political power, the revival of learning which goes under his name was centred in France and extended to parts of Germany, to Italy, Britain, and Spain. Scots and Anglo-Saxons were its leaders, and it has already been seen that they were all inspired by religious zeal and had acquired a learning which was independent of tradition. It is in this independence of tradition that the Carlovingian resembles the Italian Renaissance. The Italian scholars, from Petrarch onward, consciously reacted against medieval habits of thought and turned to the classics for direct inspiration. They succeeded beyond all expectations, and by their success broke every link with the former traditional studies, effecting a revolution the consequences of which were felt, more or less intensely, throughout western Europe.

The leaders of the Carlovingian Renaissance had different aims, for they hoped to stir up a revival of religious studies by public instruction and did not intentionally set themselves against medieval tradition; they were ignorant of and ignored tradition, and it was their good fortune that their efforts should start in France, where some traditional elements of the classical heritage still persisted, and take effect in other lands where, as particularly in Italy, the continuity of Latin tradition had never been broken.

It would be idle to enlarge upon a continuity so well known, but it would be a gross mistake to overlook it, and a few notions bearing on this point may be recalled with advantage. Where a tradition of culture did not exist there could obviously be little antagonism felt against it even by the most pious. In the lands in which, on the contrary, the old traditions had never been broken completely, such an antagonism was always apparent, and one might take it as a symptom of the persistence of tradition itself.

There had been famous teachers and men of letters in Gaul during the last days of the Roman Empire and the beginning of the Middle Ages. A poet such as Ausonius of Bordeaux (fourth century), well-read, melodious, but mostly superficial and strangely fond of trifles, is evidence, in his work as well as in his life, that there were in Gaul, as late as his age, men who were scarcely conscious of impending changes and completely satisfied in looking back to, and imitating, the forms and mannerisms of Roman literature. Christianity had no attraction for him, even though he must be reckoned a Christian. A friend of his, much praised by Augustine, is particularly interesting inasmuch as he turned entirely to the service of God, became Bishop of Nola in Italy, and openly renounced his literary studies. The position of Paulinus of Nola is the same as Augustine's : lay learning, in his opinion, was not an ill in itself, provided it were used in the service of the true Lord. To his friend Jovius he wrote: 'Change the subject of your thought and eloquence, for it is not required that your mind should renounce philosophy, provided you add to it faith and religion; you may make use of the work of the learned in order to become God's philosopher and poet.' (Ep. xvi.)

During the first half of the fifth century, when northern Gaul suffered more and more from barbaric penetration and the older traditions were restricted to the South, it was Salvian, a priest of Marseilles, who voiced a public-spirited anxiety when Cologne and Treves had been burnt by the Franks, and forecast the downfall of civilization. The style of this fifth-century Jeremiah is sufficient evidence of his learning, and his invectives against Roman corruption, together with his peculiar appreciation of the nemesis constituted by the barbaric invasions, show his keen sense of the critical stage that Europe had reached. Being completely mastered by religious zeal he could find solace only in religion; as he saw no hope for the world of his days, he turned his mind towards heaven. Despite this, his thoughts were expressed in a language that shows him to have been a student of the writers of Rome.

Not long after him, and still at Marseilles, another significant voice was heard, that of the Bishop Apollinaris Sidonius. He drew a gloomy picture of the general decay of studies, but his piety did not cause him to overlook his worldly duties. If Salvian had to flee from Cologne, Sidonius saw Marseilles occupied by the Goths. The busy life of Marseilles, the difficulties arising out of episcopal elections, the pleasures of country life and of erudition, the beginning of a kind of pacification between the Gallo-Roman population and the less recent barbaric newcomers, all these things and more are illustrated in Sidonius' letters and poems. A native of Lyons, belonging to a Christian family of wealth and repute, the son-in-law of the emperor Avitus (455), he had been trained in rhetoric and philosophy, and was so fond of writing verse that he was unable to forgo such a pleasure, despite his good intentions, when he became Bishop of Clermont-

Ferrand. It was the time when Marius Victor, himself a rhetor of Marseilles, complained:

> Barbarus incumbit; nec longa ad saecula vitae
> constructae prosunt solido de marmore villae.

Sidonius shows a wide knowledge of Latin literature and learning; his acquaintance with Greek works, on the contrary, seems to have been scant and mostly indirect, though he praised some of his friends for their familiarity with that language. On the whole he is particularly significant as illustrating a change in outlook and a deterioration in scholarship. As a patriotic citizen he was well aware of the ominous signs and dangers of the situation in his days. He observed that classical studies received less attention than heretofore, but he did not, like Salvian, urge a complete concentration on spiritual matters. On the contrary, he considered it a duty for citizens to accept public service, thus showing that he hoped for better times to come, and his laments about the literary decadence postulate his belief that an improvement was still possible. Unfortunately, the literary works of this complex man, who showed an almost unquenchable love for learning, who would scarcely allow any work of the past or of his own age to escape his attention, or any manuscripts to pass through his hands untranscribed, are evidence in themselves of a serious lowering in the standard of learning. His Latin is over-abundant in embellishments, metaphors, and even conceits; sometimes he uses Latin words in a sense different from the classical one—and it is precisely on this account that he is so significant. For deterioration is a form and a mark of continuity; quite unwillingly and unwittingly he was carried away by his environment. He admired Sallust perhaps more than other authors, because in Sallust's archaistic affectation his somewhat jaded taste found a peculiar pleasure; but when he wrote himself he was utterly unable to conform to his classical models, and he was probably unaware of his own inability.

It is a short step from Sidonius to Ennodius, another man of letters who, having become Bishop of Pavia in Lombardy (521), turned his mind entirely to religion and thereafter considered learning a danger to be carefully avoided; despite his extensive reading he was quite unable to imitate the simplicity of the classics. By this time the outlook upon the Latin language had become strangely involved: Latin was admitted to be the only possible language to use in writing and probably also in learned conversation, but in Gaul at any rate it had no longer any basis in the spoken vernacular. Thus the vernacular was a source of possible errors, and never a help, to writers; and consequently to avoid the lure of the spoken language, as occasionally recommended by late Roman grammarians, became as constant a maxim as to imitate the classical authors. The perfection of literary style seemed to be measurable merely by its remoteness from the spoken language, so that every natural form was eschewed, and complexities, alliterations, allusions, and puns were sought after. On the other hand there soon appeared works such as those of Gregory of Tours (second half of the sixth century), who was fully aware of his own lamentable ignorance of syntax and quantities, and, being untrammelled by much literary schooling, wrote in a way that but lightly dissembles a vernacular basis. His friend Venantius Fortunatus, Bishop of Poitiers, had been better trained, was better read, and possessed a better knowledge of

Latin; but his birthplace may account for his superiority, for if the schools could not be said to have escaped in Italy the effects of the barbaric invasions the classical tradition was there naturally strongest, particularly at such places as Rome and Ravenna.

The continuity of classical tradition in Italy surely needs no demonstration: Cassiodorus and Boëthius had lived and written in Italy during the sixth century, and with them Priscian and Mavortius, grammarians, and Arator, a poet; during the seventh century there wrote in Italy Gregory the Great, a writer of merit despite his grammatical imperfections, Maximianus, a Tuscan poet, Paulus Diaconus, and Peter of Pisa. The literary output may have been scant and unworthy of the classical models, but there were still schools (and probably lay as well as ecclesiastical schools); there was the practice of Roman law, which was the chosen law of the Church and for a time at least was still taught at Ravenna and Rome; there was the Roman pontiff, and above all there was Rome.

The Italians became more attached to the glories of the ancient empire as their political condition worsened, tradition taking the place of history and legend of tradition. The ancient monuments, of which incomparably larger and more conspicuous remains than those now extant were then still visible, were a constant reminder of the glorious past; and when foreigners went to visit the tomb of St. Peter, when pilgrims from distant countries—barbarians from the North who were often anxious to secure manuscripts as well as relics—reached Rome, they came under the spell of antiquity.

As early as the fourth century that charming poet Prudentius had noted the force of tradition and continuity in Rome, where heathen practices were so difficult to eradicate. If Gregory the Great lamented the decay into which the city had fallen ('quae aliquando mundi domina esse videbatur qualis remansit, Roma, conspicimus'), the poet Ausonius had still called her

> Prima urbes inter, divum domus, aurea Roma;

Alcuin himself was struck with her ruins (*de Clade Lind*. 37):

> Roma, caput mundi, mundi decus, aurea Roma,
> nunc remanet tantum saeva ruina tibi.

Another Englishman, Muadwin, was less pessimistic:

> Rursus in antiquos mutataque secula mores,
> aurea Roma iterum renovata renascitur orbi.

In later ages the impression was still the same. Thus sang the Neapolitan Vulgarius during the tenth century:

> Roma, caput mundi, rerum suprema potestas,
> terrarum terror, fulmen quod fulminat urbem,
> regnorum cultus, bellorum vivida virtus,
> immortale decus solum haec urbs super omnes.

Two centuries later Alexander Neckam wrote:

> Primitus Europae mea pagina serviet in qua
>   Roma stat, orbis apex, gloria, gemma, decus.
> Urbs titulis claris, tam laetis clara triumphis,
>   quondam bisseno Caesare tuta fuit.

And another bishop, a Frenchman, Hildebert of Lavardin, practically a contemporary of Neckam, seemed in his verses to reveal the psychological process by which the impression that Rome made grew so extraordinarily deep:

> Par tibi, Roma, nihil cum sis prope tota ruina,
>   quam magna fueris integra, fracta doces.

> .   .   .   .

> Tantum restat adhuc, tantum ruit, ut neque pars stans
>   aequari possit, diruta nec refici.

CHARLEMAGNE
from a fresco in the Vatican Galleries

See page vii

By that time the golden statues of the gods had been melted down, many monuments and buildings had been turned into quarries for marble and stone; but the power of the papal see had increased, and the recollection of Imperial Rome had been strengthened owing to the glamour surrounding the papacy and the re-established empire.

If we confine our attention to the centuries preceding the rise of Charlemagne, we ought not to overlook the reflected glamour of the Byzantine court (particularly in Southern Italy and on the coast of the Adriatic, at Naples and Ravenna), and the never suppressed influence of Roman Law, which soon affected Lombard legislation after Rothar's edict, may have been studied at Pavia in Lombard days, and had acquired a universal appeal from the moment that it became applicable to the Church. Moreover, if the already recorded dearth of literary and learned output in Italy makes it difficult to form a favourable opinion of her intellectual condition, it would be perilous to draw definite conclusions from what is after all but negative evidence. On the available evidence it would seem fairer to hold that a certain average standard of education among the lay classes was almost mechanically kept up, and that considerable activity was bestowed on practical objects,—the law, grammar, and medicine. It was a culture lacking any real vitality, but having roots too deep completely to wither.

Let us also bear in mind that scarcely any other land in western Europe, if all things are taken into account, had endured so grievous and so prolonged a torment: Goths and Greeks, Greeks and Lombards, had ceaselessly fought each other, and only during the later period of the Lombard domination, and then only in certain regions, had there been any sign in Italy of that gradual coalescence of the native and immigrant elements of the population which had been so conspicuous a feature in Spain and in France. As was to be expected, wherever the Roman tradition was strongest its suppression was more difficult, and proportionately more arduous was the inception of a new order of things. The barbarians were well able to crush an enemy in the field; but the passive and almost instinctive resistance of a population which took refuge in the cities was not to be crushed by violent means, for the citizen population was in a better position to remember and to cherish the glory and the advantages of the Roman days, and seemed to contemn the brute force of their conquerors, whom they still considered barbarians, just as they had considered their forefathers when they had served in the Roman legions. If, then, we look upon western Europe in general, it appears that, with the passing of the Visigothic power in Spain, Spain ceased for a time to play an important part in the preservation of culture; that Scots and Anglo-Saxons developed a culture of their own which for want of a better name might be described as bookish and artificial; that in France and in Italy traditional learning lasted longer, but declined in quality—style deteriorating and becoming either involved or careless, syntax and vocabulary becoming corrupt, owing to the development of the Romance vernaculars.

There had been an immense destruction of wealth, monuments, and manuscripts; there was no longer any circulating capital; trade had become primitive in its form; industrial activity had been reduced to the mere production of necessities of life. The complex organization of justice had become simplified; Germanic customs had often replaced Roman Law; the feudal system had broken up the ancient administrative organism. But, overlooking the fate of artistic monuments, the worst was over by the end of the eighth century. Capital was still practically non-existent; travel and industry were still primitive; but the network of ecclesiastical institutions was exercising an increasing influence. The Church had concentrated public education and assistance under her own direction; travel also had become a mainly religious manifestation owing to the vogue of pilgrimages; the administration of the cities tended to become an episcopal function; even architecture and art seemed to be restricted to ecclesiastical and royal buildings. A vast number of manuscripts had been destroyed; the precious vellum of old classical and religious manuscripts had been often made use of a second time by scratching out the original writing (a process which preserved a number of ancient works in the form of palimpsests), while copies in Carolingian minuscule took the place of uncial and half-uncial originals; and both palimpsests and new copies were stored in monastic and episcopal libraries. During such a process a natural selection had taken place which was accompanied by a transformation. The writers and thinkers of the first centuries of the Middle Ages had endeavoured to render heathen learning acceptable to the Christian peoples, sometimes by altering its meaning and purport, sometimes by running counter to these, and sometimes by making them subservient to religious aims. Purely lay culture was practically extinct, with the possible exception of some stray individuals and of such centres as were mainly interested in law and medicine.

Let us bear in mind that few losses of ancient works occurred after the eighth century; the main destructive epoch was over; the forces of continuity and tradition were severally operating; the materials for a revival were at hand. Scots and Anglo-Saxons provided the method and, to a certain degree, the stimulus. In France the successors of the Merovingians had achieved a political success that previous conditions seemed scarcely to warrant—internal dissensions had been suppressed, foreign enemies had been conquered, the state was strongly organized. Charlemagne was the most powerful among Western rulers; twice the popes, who no longer wished to look for protection to the Byzantine emperors, had appealed to him for help against harassing neighbours and local oppression. He was the champion of the Faith, and in the same way as he aimed at propagating Christianity among the heathens and protecting it against the Arabs he wished to secure the support of a clergy fully capable of performing its complex duties. Its inherent weakness had, however, allowed the disordered political organization of the previous period to affect the morals and the intellectual preparation of the clergy.

Fortunately for him, Charlemagne had excellent allies ready at hand. For well over a century Scots had gone to and fro throughout western Europe zealously preaching stricter morals and a sterner monastic discipline, founding monasteries and convents and assembling manuscripts of religious and secular learning. During the seventh century the monasteries of

Bobbio, St. Gall, Fleury, St.-Riquier, Péronne, and Corbie, among others, had been established by Scots. The following century saw the rise of the monastery of the Novalesa on the Alps and those of Reichenau, of Murbach, Fulda, Lorsch, in Germany, Anglo-Saxons and Scots sharing the credit. Since 772 Charlemagne himself was the ruler of the Frankish kingdom; and then, for the first time since the invasions had begun, the opportunity was afforded for interplay between the several tendencies of learning.

As early as the seventh century we learn from Virgilius Maro, the grammarian, that it was a custom to keep two separate libraries of Christian and of heathen literatures. Perhaps some notion of the kind could be drawn from Isidore of Seville's practice, but the mere mention of such a habit, whether it ever existed or not, is significant. The trouble was precisely that the two 'libraries' were too often kept separate, so that men of piety and learning took classical manuscripts from their shelves with a mixed feeling of yearning, admiration, and dread; that some of the most gifted of authors were content to base their style on the Vulgate or on earlier biblical texts and even on versions into the mixed vernacular which they happened to speak; that the less gifted and more pedantic craftsmen endeavoured to prove as strikingly difficult to their readers as the classics were difficult to them to understand. Charlemagne's political triumph and the tendencies which he encouraged caused an extraordinary change. The incidence of the Scottish and Anglo-Saxon erudition upon a literature that could show continuity of development from the ancients became effective at last. Vague aspirations received consecration in fact.

Two events seem to me particularly important: the meeting of Charlemagne with Alcuin, with all its consequences, and the imperial coronation at Rome.

The conqueror of the Saxons was a great ruler, and naturally was anxious to call to his side men capable of carrying out his plans. Learning was to him secondary: his object was the creation of a class of churchmen equal to discharging the arduous duties which their calling and his policy thrust upon them; corruption and vice, he had realized, had one of their principal sources in ignorance. He was no doubt aware of the zeal of the Scots who had followed in Columban's tracks and some of whom had become more or less established within the boundaries of his states; he was aware of the energy with which the Anglo-Saxon Boniface and Willibord had pursued his object of converting the Germans to Christianity; and at Parma, in 780, he met Alcuin. This learned head of the York school he had probably known already in 768 at Aix-la-Chapelle, and he was anxious to secure the assistance of a man whose organizing capability must have been as outstanding as his learning. The king had taken a daring step. Instead of trusting in a revival of monastic and episcopal schools, he established a school of the palace, a school which was to move about with the court and thus to remain under the immediate eye of the sovereign, who, being familiar with colloquial Latin at any rate, took a particular interest in religious studies. Just as he wished to organize his state, he was anxious to strengthen the hierarchical discipline of the Church; under his rule the authority of migrating Irish bishops received a setback, and it waned during the ninth century. So great was his influence in ecclesiastical matters and so active was his pursuit of orderliness that it has been asserted that the Roman Missal as arranged by Gregory the Great and variously modified by the Visigoths of Spain and by the Scots, particularly in France, received its present form during and after Charlemagne's reign, possibly through Alcuin himself.

What characterized Alcuin, even more than his extended learning and his wide reading, especially in patristic literature, was his scholarly instinct. He was a well-trained Latinist, and in point of fact his principal work deals with grammar; when he wrote, he used Latin with ease and perspicuity, conforming, as exactly as his knowledge allowed, to classical standards. He realized that learning was in jeopardy; much had been lost in extent and depth of scholarship on the Continent. He knew that some of his predecessors in England had been compelled to cross the Irish Channel for instruction; he had himself travelled to Rome before 780, probably with a view also to enriching the conspicuous store of books which were preserved at York; and from the moment that he became responsible for the direction of the Palace school he never ceased to collect books from Italy and England, taking care that they should be transcribed in the elegant and clear hand which had developed in recent years—probably in France—and properly punctuated and revised. The so-called Carlovingian minuscule does not owe its origin to him, but he must have realized its merits; for he showed constant interest in the technical means by which scholarship could be perfected and transmitted to later ages.

Just as he collected books, he endeavoured to gather around himself eminent men who might help him. This organized and royally fostered effort brought about a rapid revival of learning, no doubt; but every revival implies death, and Latin, once a spoken and traditional language, becomes for the first time a dead language, when the well-trained scholars of the court of Charlemagne started to use it with almost classical accuracy and taste. Einhard was to model his life of the sovereign on Suetonius; and it happened that the Emperor found it necessary to command the clergy to employ a less classical Latin style in the discharge of their ecclesiastical duties lest misunderstandings occurred.

Alcuin, an Anglo-Saxon, was succeeded by Clement, a Scot, in the direction of the Palace school. Einhard was a German and a man of extraordinary parts; Theodulph was a Goth; Charlemagne had, it seems, learned some Greek from old Peter of Pisa, who was perhaps an Italian; Greek was taught for a time at the Court by a Lombard who hailed from and had been trained in Italy, Paulus Warnefridi, better known as Paulus Diaconus, the author of the *Historia Langobardorum*. The sentiments which these men endeavoured to express had little in them that was ancient; they were Saxons, Scots, Germans, and Lombards, men belonging to races which had no part in Latin culture and which had contibuted to its downfall. Charlemagne considered learning a means to the training of an efficient clergy; his aims were political and religious. Alcuin in the midst of his labours still thought with regret of his cell at York:

> O mea cella, mihi habitatio dulcis, amata,
> semper in aeternum, o mea cella, vale.

It is notable that these churchmen and politicians acquired some of the mannerisms which Petrarch and the Italian humanists were so often to affect: they described one another with classical nicknames, Naso, Homerus, etc.; but the world of their thoughts remained medieval and Christian; this was their strength and their weakness. A complete reversal of values could only take place in the country where tradition was strongest, among people who, rightly or wrongly, considered the Romans their ancestors.

In this respect the circumstances of Charlemagne's coronation are particularly interesting. When the power of the king of the Franks grew so that all the rulers of his age looked up to him, as earlier sovereigns had looked up to Theoderic the Goth, the idea of the imperial coronation was mooted. The new world was being linked with the ancient; but the new world did not at first look with favour on the revival of an ancient authority to which the Franks felt racially averse, and Einhard would have it that the pope thrust the honour by surprise upon an unwilling king. Whatever the trustworthiness of this account, it must be noted that the coronation took place in Italy, at Rome, and by the hand of the pope, the head of an institution which had taken over much of what used to be among the attributes of the ancient empire. The *translatio imperii* was to have important consequences, but was in itself a triumph of tradition over force. Many adventurers, many uncouth soldiers had been raised to the throne during the last centuries of the Roman Empire; from a practical angle the opponents were right who maintained that the new title would not add to the power of the king of the Franks; its value consisted entirely in the value which was given to it, and this was based on tradition. If the force of tradition had not been operating, it would have been idle to call Charlemagne Emperor of Rome, as it was an idle affectation for Angilbert to call himself Homer and for Theodulph to be known as Pindar.

The event took place at Rome, where the ancient monuments compelled an almost superstitious awe; and once the step had been taken, it was realized that the force of tradition was bound to rank itself by the side of the Emperor. His authority was *ipso facto* rendered legitimate; the majestic tradition of Roman Law became an ally of the Emperor. And as the study of Roman Law had been taken up in the Palace school, it had probably persisted, in however rudimentary a form, in the schools of Italy. It would appear that at the beginning of the ninth century, thanks to the will of the Emperor, the school of Pavia was founded. Dungal the Scot had been sent to Pavia, and an edict had been proclaimed which aimed at reviving studies in Italy. This edict is not evidence in itself that its objects were attained, but there are documents which seem to point to a certain success.

The co-ordination of efforts which the Emperor had rendered possible lasted, however, little longer than Charlemagne's life; and the so-called Carlovingian Renaissance ended as rapidly as it had begun. Some works which were produced under its influence, such as Einhard's *Vita Karoli*, are remarkable; some poems are graceful, but no one fully succeeded in wedding the medieval spirit to classical forms; and the importance of this epoch should be sought in the impetus it gave to study, the foundation of schools, and the transcription of manuscripts.

Of all these perhaps the transcription of manuscripts

was in its effects the most lasting achievement. The adoption of a finer script, the use of classical nicknames, the effort to imitate Augustan models, even the stripping of Ravenna and Rome of their marbles to decorate the palace at Aix-la-Chapelle ('ad cuius structuram, cum columnas et marmora aliunde habere non posset, Roma atque Ravenna devehenda curavit'—Einhard, 26), were after all externals. The heart of Charlemagne remained with his race and with his native language. It is Einhard again who tells us: 'Item barbara et antiquissima carmina, quibus veterum regum actus et bella canebantur, scripsit memoriaeque mandavit. Inchoavit et grammaticam patrii sermonis' (Einhard, 29).

The spirit was still medieval, but meanwhile all the works that could be traced had been transcribed, and practically all that we know of the writers of Rome goes back solely or mainly to Carlovingian copies.

Nothing was lost, and yet little had been truly found. Cicero and Virgil were read, Tacitus and Suetonius were imitated, but they and their contemporaries were not fully understood. There are two ways by which the classical legacy can make itself felt: as a formal survival imposing ancient manners of expression upon new thoughts and new feelings (and this is the less effective if the more obviously striking), or as a source by tapping which medieval thought could be enriched. Classical learning could not be assimilated unless it became modified. A modification by curtailment and simplification had taken place during the earlier Middle Ages, but the process of rediscovery had run counter to it, and it was a procedure, at best, which was too matter-of-fact to be satisfying. To be able to read such of the works of the Romans as had not been destroyed, to know the things that they said, was not to understand them. The classics were gazed upon, but did not look down upon their admirers; they were imitated, no doubt, but they did not speak. In scientific matters the Carlovingian scholars were childishly puzzled; in philosophy they were just feeling their way and groping about.

This was a result perhaps of the loss of Greek as distinct from Roman culture; for out of it all there emerges a fact that cannot be overlooked. The knowledge of Greek, even if we believed Einhard, who, imitating Suetonius, would like us to give credit to his hero for the possession of that language, was restricted to a very few, and despite the presence of Byzantine monks in southern Italy was on the verge of completely disappearing. Greece spoke to the Middle Ages only with the voice of Rome; and Rome had impressed her stamp upon Greek culture so as considerably to alter its character.

In recent years the originality of the Latin genius has been challenged with great decision and much persistence. It is of comparatively little importance to the student of the Middle Ages to decide whether some of the ideas which characterized Roman culture were due to the influence of pre-Roman elements in Italy, to Roman citizens of non-Roman descent, or to the acceptance of foreign and mainly Eastern influences. Whatever their origin, they became acclimatized in the Roman world, were accepted as Roman, and, because they were Roman and held to be Roman, they kept the Middle Ages under their spell. Greek culture ceased to exist, and its tendencies were only recaptured much later; they necessarily had to be transplanted into a field that was completely Roman, even though it had been adapted to the new conditions.

VII

THE SCHOOLMEN AND AFTER

IN some ways one of the most lasting consequences of the Carlovingian Renaissance was totally unlooked for. The works of ancient philosophers had been familiar to many an early Father of the Church, and many a Platonic idea was transmitted by Augustine to the Middle Ages; but the disorganization and the wars that prepared and followed upon the downfall of Rome did not only stunt literary output and scientific investigation, they also suppressed philosophic speculation or made it merely formal and timid. To what purpose would men have investigated the secret of life when Christian revelation provided a complete answer to this as well as to all other problems? The larger problem, the ultimate and all-important problem, was settled for ever. The works of the ancients, or such of them as were studied, were explicitly regarded as being under suspicion. If and where they seemed to run counter to Christian doctrine, they were to be condemned and avoided as dangerous. Ancient metaphysical conceptions, even if known, could have no attraction. There were, however, other books of ancient learning, seemingly unconnected with the search for ultimate truth, that afforded considerable help in the process of understanding lesser and subsidiary points in the field of philosophy—books on logic, dialectic, and so on. From Boëthius to Isidore, and from Isidore to Alcuin, philosophy as we understand it had been mostly replaced by the strictly-classified liberal arts—Grammar, Rhetoric, and Dialectic forming the

Trivium, Arithmetic, Geometry, Astronomy, and Music constituting the *Quadrivium*. Knowledge was to be reached by a careful study of the Arts (on practical grounds Medicine was soon to creep in among them, though Law was long kept apart); all together they were supposed to comprise, and in some way to lead to, philosophy. A few stray philosophical concepts were traceable here and there, but ultimately philosophy was subservient to theology, and thus every transcendental idea was strictly within the domain of theology and severely subordinate to it.

In general this may be taken as true for the Carlovingian period; but it was precisely during that period that a new organization of studies had taken place. Schools had been founded, classical manuscripts had been rendered more accessible by copies, and thus the data were provided from which an original intellect might proceed to the disquieting realization of problems that the ancients had not only stated but solved— solved, however, in a way which was not easily reconcilable with Christianity.

The care bestowed on education rendered the arising of such an eventuality more probable; scholars, however, were almost exclusively to be found among churchmen. And thus this realization may have been retarded by the straightened discipline of the Church and at the same time made more poignant when it arose. Up to the days of Charlemagne learning had been undergoing a process by which it was simplified and systematized to suit the debased standard of culture; it was planned so as to render a man of learning equally competent in all departments; the encyclopaedic habit became characteristic of the Middle Ages. Needless to say, each of the leading men possessed, despite this, his own intellectual individuality; and there were men whose preferences turned to literature, while others excelled in grammar or theology, in music or medicine. Hence arose a variety which was at one and the same time natural and puzzling. These medieval men felt immeasurably superior to the ancients, because of the transcendental faith which they possessed, as they felt inferior to the old masters in stylistic craftsmanship, in science, and in learning. Their feeling of inferiority was increased rather than impaired by their studies. In literary matters—in style, in grammar, in dialectic, rhetoric, and so on—their ultimate goal was only to recapture a glory and a perfection which had been reached by the ancients and was obtainable no longer: it was a hopeless form of antiquarianism, when it was not aided by original power; imitation was the ultimate standard of perfection. In literature, however, an intense study of classical models, well chosen, could promote literary sensibility and the power of expressing a new world of thought in a language that, though based on classical models, possessed some added elements and was transformed in accordance with the spirit of the age. In the field of philosophy and science, on the contrary, wider knowledge compelled the realization of the profound chasm which separated ancient thought from Christian conceptions. Such a realization might cause the less daring and more pious to recoil from the heathen past, as Jerome had recoiled. And yet it was felt that it would bring about a grievous loss to condemn ancient learning because of its heathen implications. In order fully to reconquer classical thought, it became necessary to eliminate its heathen characteristics—after all, the ancients, though heathen, had been created by the true God, and thus what was best in their thoughts could not be irreducible to God's truth. It was precisely this process of understanding and thus christianizing ancient philosophy, in so far as it had been transmitted, that became characteristic of the period following upon the Carlovingian era.

Already the German pupil of Alcuin, Rabanus Maurus (776–856), among his many works based on those of his master, seemed to aim at recasting works by other writers which had been famous during the early Middle Ages, such as Isidore's *Etymologies*, with a closer attention to, and a stronger bias in favour of, theology. But at most he was a forerunner. The great initiator of the movement was John the Scot (*c.* 805–*c.* 875), an Irishman by birth. This remarkable man possessed a fair knowledge of Greek, and translated the works of Dionysius the Areopagite into Latin. In writing about predestination against Gotteschalk, and in his work *De Divisione Naturae*, he was the first among the schoolmen who attempted a philosophical conspectus of the Universe; he was influenced by neo-Platonism and was more attracted by the Greek than by the Latin Fathers. Holding that reason and theology derived from God's wisdom, he established their equality and thus their identity: true philosophy was true religion. Following Augustine, he ascribed to authority no more value than to reason, for authority 'is simply the established result of reason, the reason being prior in essence to authority'.

It was to be expected that a philosopher who so confidently trusted in reason as a means of interpreting dogmas would fall foul of ecclesiastical authority, and the controversy between him and his opponents 'may well be regarded as the turning-point in the history of medieval scholarship'. It was owing to him that the Greek spirit of inquiry was transplanted into the study of Christian religion, and his instinctive antagonism to the mechanical tradition of Rome was evinced by his admiration for the Eastern Empire.

> Constantinopolis florens nova Roma vocatur,
> Moribus et muris Roma vetusta cadis.
> Transiit imperium, mansitque superbia tecum,
> Cultus avaritiae te nimium superat.

This undaunted man, the influence of whose works was to be felt for centuries to come and to help in bringing about a revival of philosophical learning in the West, seems to have championed the East. His importance was not fully realized at the time, but an instinctive feeling of it would appear to be shown by the legendary anecdotes which cropped up about him. The manner of his death is surrounded by mystery: according to Malmesbury, he was stabbed to death by his pupils with their pens. The same source recounts that when John was at the court of Charles the Bald he was asked by the Emperor during a meal, 'quid distat inter Scottum et Sottum?', and replied, tabula tantum.' John the Scot was the first of the schoolmen deeply to probe into the question of the universals, the importance of which his predecessors had felt rather than understood. Boëthius had transmitted to the Middle Ages the ancient questions propounded by Porphyry. 'Do the genera and species exist in nature or only in our thought? If they exist in nature, have they a bodily existence, and do they exist as separate from perceptible things or in the things themselves?' The solution of such a problem implied the construction of a complete system of philosophy. And soon the philosophical field was divided among nominalists and realists; but apart from John the Scot the great exponents of this question were not to be found before the eleventh century, and even Gerbert, who appeared to be so great to his contemporaries, quite as much because of his learning as because of their ignorance, did not usefully re-examine this tremendous problem.

The disasters which befell western Europe during the tenth century—wars and renewed invasions—caused the benefits of the Carlovingian revival of learning to remain dormant. They were dormant but not lost. It was then, probably, that the knowledge of Greek was everywhere suppressed in the West except in southern Italy. The organization of study which had been established was put out of gear, and France suffered so much that she seemed to slip from the pre-eminent position that she had hitherto occupied. Germany, where the Saxon Emperor had strengthened the constitution of the feudal empire, became the centre around which learning revolved. At the Court of the Ottos, at Aix-la-Chapelle, Bruno held sway; a northern from Liège, Ratherius, the restless Bishop of Verona, showed extraordinary independence of spirit and conduct. In France, beside some Scottish foundations which helped to preserve learning from a complete disaster, there was founded the monastery of Cluny (910), whose influence was soon to extend to allied houses of the Order; but these pious monks strictly considered learning as secondary to religious zeal. It was in Germany that an attempt was also made at substituting plays consistent with Christian morality for the heathen and 'immoral' Terence, and the attempt was made by that remarkable nun Hroswitha. In Italy, then as earlier and later, there were laymen as well as ecclesiastics of learning, and it happened not rarely that their learning was rather dependent on tradition than concerned with religious concepts. From Verona there hailed a little jewel,

> O Roma nobilis, orbis et domina,
> cunctarum urbium excellentissima,

which seems to be entirely due to traditional inspiration. A poem permeated with classical mythology is ascribed to the soldiers watching on the walls of Modena. That adventurous and restless monk, Radulphus Glaber, tells an interesting story of about 1030, which may not be true in fact, but must still be considered as significant because of its implications. A certain Vilgardus of Ravenna, a most zealous student of 'grammatica', 'as Italians are wont to be who take little care of the other arts and only study grammar', was tempted by demons who cunningly appeared to him in the shape of Virgil, Horace, and Juvenal, with the result that the unhappy man, fired by the hope of sharing in the glory of his beloved poets, lapsed into heresy. It is a piece of evidence that might perhaps be overlooked if it lacked corroboration, particularly if it is taken into account that Glaber proceeded to refer to the spread of heresy to Sardinia and to Spain, pointing out that these horrors had been pre-announced in the *Apocalypse* of St. John. But what Wipo of Burgundy wrote about the high standard of education in Italy, what we know about the existence of schools and book-production in that country, and what must be inferred about the beginnings of legal studies at Pavia and Bologna, jointly convince us that, if the literary output seems to have been scant, enthusiastic admirers of classical authors were fairly frequent among Italians. A typical teacher of rhetoric was Eugenius Vulgarius of Naples, and a strange representative of this class, a man of letters pure and simple, must have been Gunzo of Novara, who possessed the vanity and susceptibility of an Italian humanist of the Renaissance. Having been scoffed at by a young monk of Saint Gall, when on his way to the Imperial court, for using an accusative instead of an ablative in his speech, he urged the irrelevance of such a reproach; for 'being wont to use a vernacular very close to Latin, he, as well as his countrymen, was liable to make such slips' despite his extraordinary learning, on the extent of which he abundantly enlarges, mentioning also that he was taking to Germany more than a hundred manuscripts. Something of the same pride in their encyclopaedic learning and in their books was shown by Anselm of Besate and Benedict of Chiusa, who, according to Ademar of Chabannes, proclaimed: 'Habeo duas magnas domos plenas libris'. Italy was still the place whence manuscripts were imported, according also to the evidence of Gerbert, who wrote (Epistle 130): 'Nosti quot scriptores in urbibus aut agris Italiae passim habeantur.' Gerbert of Auvergne had been brought up in the school of Cluny and was thus concerned with the moral reform of the clergy; but, having studied in Spain, having been Abbot of Bobbio, and having lived at the Saxon court and been Bishop of Ravenna, he had great opportunities of satisfying his thirst for learning. In fact his reading included, besides many classical and religious authors, works on medicine, mathematics, and music. In the history of science he is accorded an important place, but otherwise his contribution to learning would appear to have been conservative rather than creative. He was fully aware that Norman and Hungarian invasions had wrought havoc also in the field of studies, and, following in the steps of the pioneers in the earlier Middle Ages, he strove to preserve as much as he could of ancient learning from loss and destruction.

The real revival was however approaching, and was to be the work of the great schoolmen. So far, through the stimulus of tradition and the force of traditional institutions—of the Church and the Schools, the memory of past glories and the monuments of ancient Rome, the admiration for the classics in a few, and the needs of ritual and legislation—the effort had been principally conservative. It was civilization struggling for survival against a twofold attack: the attack of the barbaric races instinctively antagonistic to Rome and primarily destructive, and the ecclesiastical attack prompted by the consciousness that classical learning was not reducible to Christian standards. The ruins of Rome as described by Hildebert may as well symbolize the amount of the loss. Despite this, the spirit of Rome, which is to say of civilization, had conquered all along. Theoderic and Charlemagne showed that the kings of the new peoples themselves might become the champions of tradition. Charlemagne and the Saxon emperors possibly lacked a clear perception of the mission they were fulfilling. Manuscripts had to be saved, churches erected, discipline restored. Discipline implied organization and order, and therefore legislation—Roman law permeating and supplanting traditional law; a uniform ritual taking the place of the prevailing anarchy. Law and order required schools: and schools of law, for instance, would perforce have to go back to the Justinian Codex. The effort was practical rather than speculative; the stress was too great to allow people to discern any but the surface difficulties. The subtleties of legal interpretation and procedure escaped them, just as they were still unaware of the essence of classical art. They were conscious of their own inferiority as compared with the ancient poets, and thus considered imitation the only way to salvation. Of the deadening effect of imitation they had, of course, no conception; but, unfortunately for them, imitation can only be successful when based on a correct understanding, whereas Virgil was to them a magician and sage, and Ovid a moralist. Their aims and their theoretical basis were all wrong: and yet their practice was sometimes right, for they succeeded in expressing their feelings and thoughts.

And there was another force at work in the field of literature and art. Practical needs, religious and military, imposed certain conditions on architects who had consciously to depart from classical models; and the new ecclesiastical buildings called for decorations which could seldom be imitated from the ancients. It was the same in the study and practice of law, where new conditions imposed continuous adaptations and modifications of Roman edicts. And the people who could not refrain from voicing in verse their loves and their pride, their religious emotions and their historical legends, had found other vehicles than the stilted language of the learned.

The new languages were not the foes but became the rivals of Latin, and rivals more deadly than foes; for

Latin survived as the language of learning, sometimes as the medium of emotional expression when the writer happened pre-eminently to be a man of learning; but as a rule it was a language into which the full breath of life was ceasing or had ceased to flow. It is a proof of the tremendous force of tradition that Latin should have survived so long. It would seem gallantly to have kept up a semblance of life until all the new languages had risen to literary rank. Yet one dare not mistake the semblance of life for life itself. Creative literature, the literature of poets in the etymological meaning of the word, found readier means of expression in the Germanic and Romance vernaculars. From the open fields, where the sun shines and the wind blows, Latin withdrew into the churches, the tribunals, the schools, and the scriptoria of the learned. In these surroundings, however, it was treated almost as a living language, and was, with certain qualifications, a living language; particularly because the brotherhood of the learned and the universality of culture were never more keenly realized. And the powerful organization of the Church never seemed more all-pervading.

One needs to remember what has already been stated, that until the gleanings of the Italian scholars of the Renaissance, and with the exception of certain books of Aristotle's, after the Carlovingian period no classical work was rescued from oblivion. That period saw the crowning effort at, and the triumph of, conservation. Later on, deeper problems faced the scholars. The question was no longer how to understand the literal meaning of the classics, but to reconcile them with Christianity and the new world which had arisen and was arising from the ruins of the ancient world.

John the Scot had shown that there were difficulties which ancient philosophers had tackled and which had to be tackled afresh from another angle. Men whose minds were troubled by problems so deep could not dally in choosing a word, in measuring their sentences by the standard of classical examples. Under the pressure of thought, style often departed from classicism, and Latin gained for this very reason a new lease of life. Theirs was not the barbarism of ignorance so much as the daring of men anxious to deliver a message of truth and therefore unwilling to be restrained by formal rules.

Into the subtleties of philosophical speculation it is not our purpose to go. During the eleventh century philosophical studies had made considerable strides. From Italy, where, as has been mentioned already, a certain tradition of purely literary activity had never completely been broken, there hailed two luminaries who were destined to leave a deep impress upon the culture of the epoch: Lanfranc, who was first educated at Pavia but pursued his main philosophical studies at Bec in Normandy and became Archbishop of Canterbury, and Anselm of Aosta, who closely followed in his steps and succeeded him at Canterbury—Lanfranc, who never fully condemned the reading of classical authors, but in philosophy never allowed reason to rival authority, and Anselm, a man of profound intellect and unshakable faith, who stood adamant against all contemporary attempts at subjecting the sacred books to the interpretative methods of dialectic. Faith in God is the necessary premise to intellectual advancement; 'credo ut intelligam' was his motto; but once faith was acquired, it would have been, according to him, negligence not to re-examine that which men believed they understood. Within such limits he constructed a theory of God and of transcendental truth, and thus gave a direction to scholasticism which was long followed. The opposite tendency was championed by Berengarius of Tours, who considered dialectic an excellent instrument for the understanding of divine truth.

There is some danger, however, of forgetting the realities of general culture when focussing one's attention on the greatest exponents of scholarship and investigation. Latin culture in its purity had taken shelter in the schools, but even among the schoolmen there were few who could fully and immediately appreciate the import of the divergences between Anselm of Aosta and Berengarius or Roscellinus, fewer still who were able to add anything original to their speculation. Their voices were to find an echo only among the most prominent of their contemporaries and among some of their followers. Despite this, once problems so fundamental had been stated, even the teaching of humble professionals could not remain quite unaltered; their methods were gradually affected, and room had to be found for philosophy in the regular curriculum of studies, which was bound to conform to the general principles that each individual teacher adopted.

The rise of vernacular literature tended to restrict the field in which Latin was pre-eminent, and thus also tended to engender, in those who wrote in Latin, a feeling of remoteness, and of what I should call, for want of a better word, academicism. Their very medium of expression helped them to realize that the subject with which they dealt was remote from the men of the people and was intended for a select public of readers. Conversely it could, and often did, render these scholars sensitive about their mastery of the medium they used, and even irritated by the attention which readers might give to their literary merits as distinct from their scholarly attainments and religious zeal.

Peter Damiani, a most eloquent and ardent Church reformer, trembled with indignation at the thought that his works might be studied rather for the sake of their literary merit than on account of any real interest in the moral reforms which he advocated. His piety caused him to abominate the very idea of classical studies, while Lanfranc consented to a guarded study of even heathen authors, and Berengarius was averse to the 'auctores' in general. His was a most interesting attitude: he accepted the Middle Ages and refused to go back to their sources. Since the Arts existed and were taught, it was immaterial to investigate whence they had sprung. Priscian, Donatus, and Boëthius had taught grammar and logic to the Middle Ages: well and good, it behoved now these scholars to study the Arts as they were—that is to say as they had been formulated after successive modifications, leaving Boëthius and Priscian alone. It was a modernist movement which implied a rebellion against, or at least a departure from, 'authority' as represented by the 'auctores'; and the school of Chartres reacted against it. The original merit of the sources was championed there, as against the doubtful advantages of a naturally developed tradition; as a consequence which was not looked for, some of the admirers of the 'auctores' insensibly approached near to the style of their models, and their Latin was as comparatively pure and classical as John of Salisbury's, himself a disciple of Chartres.

It is well, however, to look beyond the most striking effects of such contrasts. In a sense the conflict between the champions of the 'auctores' and the champions of the Arts was a phase of the constant conflict between the ancients and the moderns—between the return to the past, intended rather than achieved, and the aspiration to a new perfection to be attained in the future.

Every form of renaissance arises from a reactionary stimulus and, when successful, concludes with a forward stride. In so far as they felt confidence in their own knowledge and intellectual powers, and were willing to measure their own achievements by new standards, men were progressive; and they refused submissively to obey either authority in intellectual speculation or the 'auctores' in literary studies. Contrariwise, when the awe caused by divine inspiration triumphed over their reliance on the power of reason, and when the appreciation of, and admiration for, ancient masterpieces filled them with humility and with doubts as to their own powers, scholars returned to the originals.

The great change which had taken place since the earlier Middle Ages was that the savage elements of destruction had been checked, tamed, and forced into obedience. In the early days there was on one side Rome in her faded if solemn glory, echoing as much of Greek thought and art as she had assimilated, and on the other side the brutal force of the barbarians, some of whom could not brook any sense of inferiority towards the Romans and tried to establish an unchallenged supremacy either by acquiring or by destroying Latin culture. Both attempts had conspired to produce a similar effect; culture was impaired in quantity by the latter and in quality by the former; it was deadened and simplified so as to bring it down to the level which the average man could reach. The few heroes who stood out as champions of civilization could do no more than refashion as much as was possible of ancient knowledge in a form suitable to the new environment. Now, when the Middle Ages were coming to a close, even the last barbarian settlers had been checked or assimilated—checked, as the Hungarians, or assimilated, as the Normans. Among the most ardent and proficient exponents of learning and speculation were men whose ancestors had contributed to the destruction of civilization. The purely conservative stage was over and the great struggle was at an end. So far there had been little which could be considered a medieval contribution; and that little was, directly or indirectly, based on the ancients. Life and its manifestations were moving away into new tracks. While old buildings were falling into ruins, castles were erected on the hills and in the country, churches and monasteries vied in massive magnificence with the feudal structures, and, later, town-halls represented in their grandeur the rising power and ambitions of the cities. The warlike inhabitants of the castles and their cowed subjects ceased to understand Latin; the rise of many different languages to literary rank signified the downfall of the ideal of universality and the breaking-up of the feudal system which had been its last political expression. Love and hatred, holy legends and warlike epics, were sung in the different languages. Of course the transition was gradual; for a time the Germanic languages were close enough to their original form to be but slightly differentiated, and the Romance languages seemed to be almost interchangeable. Many a poet chose to write in a dialect which he had not originally spoken, and often poets would compose, indifferently or successively, in more than one language.

At a first glance it would appear as though continuity were broken, and it is undeniable that the passing of time and the natural course of events were bringing new forces into play—fundamental feelings, which could not undergo a change, received new forms of expression. Against these changes the forces of continuity could claim victories in other fields. The very idea of a universal Empire owed its origin and cogency rather to the recollection of Roman glories than to the ambition of the barbaric sovereigns. And parallel to a universal Empire there was established a universal Church, no less dependent on Roman traditions. The emperors endeavoured to administer justice in accordance with Roman Law, and above the confusion of customary laws there stood forth the laws collected by Justinian— laws which were formulated in Latin and interpreted and commented in Latin. In Latin also the Christians prayed and worshipped; and the ecclesiastical laws (Canons) were as Latin in language as they were Roman in inspiration.

Even architecture and the arts owed much to ancient tradition and models. Einhard, an architect as well as a scholar and statesman, was a close student of Vitruvius, and it is easier to assert than to prove that medieval architecture and art were dependent on few, and remote, Eastern models rather than on the almost countless examples of Roman art. The manifold manifestations of a new creative spirit render the study of the later much more complex than that of the earlier Middle Ages. It is more difficult, therefore, to detect their common ground. Despite this, it is well to remember that, however little the general public be aware of it, there are certain ideas which may be considered characteristic of each age; and it is the function of philosophers, thinkers, and, in a wide sense, men of letters, to formulate and express these ideas. Even the most original of philosophers owes something to his environment. Philosophers may anticipate later developments, and thus be credited with the merit of causing them, or merely identify and co-ordinate the intellectual foundations of political and social events in their own days. In either case they provide a precious key to the understanding of far-off epochs. And medieval philosophy remained in form Latin. The schoolmen endeavoured, as we have seen, to interpret in Christian terms that which the ancients had thought; there were pioneers among them who struck out on dangerous paths, there were men to whom considerable originality could not be denied. But fate seemed against originality. When the Middle Ages had absorbed, modified, and interpreted what little was left of ancient culture and philosophy, contact with the Arabs brought new books of Aristotle into the light; and the work of christianization had to be taken up afresh.

During the early part of the twelfth century the remaining sections of Aristotle's *Organon* began to be noticed by scholars; the *Physics* and *Metaphysics* circulated some decades later, probably about 1200. For the first time medieval men were confronted with a complete philosophic system; and, if their methods did not undergo a thorough change, the range of their knowledge and the importance of the problems discussed greatly increased. There followed first a period of assimilation and then a period of christianization, which was concluded by the works of Albert of Cologne and Thomas Aquinas.

The philosophic activity seemed to have its natural home in France. Whatever the nationality of the scholars, and whatever the sources of their new speculations, it cannot be gainsaid that the University of Paris became more and more the centre to which philosophical ideas tended, and from which they moved out to the conquest of western Europe.

There are some points which need, however, to be remembered: the new influx of knowledge was ultimately of Greek origin and the Western scholars knew no Greek; they were forced to avail themselves of translations, mostly translations at second hand which were made in Spain and in other regions where Eastern and Western scholarship came into contact. Greek was destined to remain a mysterious language, the secret of which was the desire of many, but was granted to no Western scholar to possess. According to Roger Bacon, John Grosseteste procured teachers of Greek from Southern Italy, where Basilian monasteries and Byzantine traditions existed; but these early efforts proved of scant success. A Church Council ordered Greek and Hebrew to be studied; but it is certain that Greek was little better known than Hebrew, and Hebrew was not known at all.

It was so difficult to break away from the purely Latin tradition that even the works of Aristotle could not be considered as sure possessions until they were clothed in the Latin language. Meanwhile, Latin itself, as the language of learning, was studied. Once again the field was divided into two parties—the philosophers pure and simple who affected to despise mere literary proficiency, and the men of letters, whose principal merit was a certain ability in making use of the Latin language. Of all-round scholars, men who were equally at home in philosophical discussion and in composing choice pieces of Latin modelled on a favourite classic, there was perhaps one only, John of Salisbury. Even such men as made a particular study of the Roman language, who devised rules of versification and compiled anthologies for the guidance of people less proficient than themselves, were anxious to show their ability in a higher field. They preached against the debased style of the purely philosophical schoolmen, they inveighed against the vices of medieval versification, but their own style seldom rose above mediocrity. No doubt the philosophers were the worst offenders, for they despised the 'authors' as much as those men of earlier days had despised them who lived in fear of their heathen attractions, and, framing their style on biblical Latin and on the new translations from the Arabic and Hebrew, departed completely from the classical standards. They dealt with Latin as if Latin were a living language, and thus renounced all the advantages that a literary training could afford; so that only when a man of surpassing genius appeared, who was so absorbed in his reading as to be almost secluded from life—a man therefore for whom Latin had actually become a second language—could eloquence of diction be recognized in his works. Aquinas, a little later, was the most perfect representative of this class. As for the

THE EMPEROR JUSTINIAN

from the mosaics in the church of S. Vitale at Ravenna

See page viii

others, they were still conscious of their own inferiority and anxious to learn from a close study of the classics, and consequently aimed at the revival of a partly dead language; but they lacked the power to raise themselves above the tendencies of their own age, and they also lacked the critical insight which was necessary to an accurate evaluation of classical craftsmanship. Their works were mosaics of quotations, and their style was stilted and notable for rhetorical artifice rather than finish.

In Italy, however, where the marks of Roman greatness were still more conspicuous than elsewhere, new signs soon became apparent. The country had suffered much during the preceding centuries, but the native population had easily assimilated the settlers of earlier periods, and had successfully antagonized the Hohenstauffen emperors; in the course of that struggle many had been the expressions of sentiments that we should now identify with national feeling. Side by side with national feeling there had developed national traits in culture and intellectual life, among them a practical tendency in the field of learning. Pure speculation was considered an appurtenance of Paris; there were philosophers of course among Italians, but these philosophers were mostly educated, and sometimes lived and taught, in France, from Anselm of Aosta and Lanfranc to Aquinas and Marsilius of Padua. The school of Salerno, closely connected with Eastern learning, had specialized in medicine; the other Italian universities made law their principal subject of study. Bologna spelt law as Paris philosophy. Law of course meant Roman Law, and thus an immediate contact with one of the institutions on which the Roman genius had left its strongest mark, and with documents and books which were the record of the legal genius of Rome. Since Irnerius, if not before, the study of law had implied the interpretation and minute comment of the original edicts contained in the Justinian Code. The legal phraseology of the Romans was no doubt far removed from the smooth *concinnitas* of Cicero, but it exemplified the Latin of ancient Rome in its force and purity. It was consequently but natural that, as a preparation for, and a department of, the study of law, the study and the practice of grammar and rhetoric should flourish. Irnerius himself seems to have progressed to the teaching of law from the teaching of grammar.

Moreover, in Italy, up to the thirteenth century, the local vernaculars had not attained literary recognition; and thus Latin was there, more than elsewhere, almost a living language, for the occasions for its use were many; and with a view to providing for a large circle of pupils, of lay pupils in particular, the school of Bologna followed a practice which had already found some favour elsewhere, notably at Monte Cassino, and fostered the compilation of books in which masters gave examples for the various occasions which arose in official and private correspondence and speech-making. These collections (*Summa artis dictandi*, *Dictamen*) soon gained a wide circulation. Their main interest, besides the historical information which they occasionally impart to us, lies in the conscious attempt to suit the style to the occasion, and thus to be in turns involved, artificial, and fairly simple. Their style is almost consistently inelegant and their phraseology often redolent of vernacular idiom, and it would truly be difficult to trace any classical influence in them. Despite this, the compilation of such models of letters and speeches, and the intellectual attitude which such works postulated, bore, in my opinion, considerable fruit. A few of these students of law became fired by the wish to penetrate more deeply into the secret of the ancient authors. The vernacular dialects were now spoken everywhere, and those students who meant to write Latin occasionally felt the need to conform to classical rather than more recent examples. They must have begun to realize, if still obscurely, that Latin was not really their native language; and such an obscure feeling must have existed despite their traditional conviction that it was. They called themselves 'Latini', they were students of Roman Law, they were taught in the schools no other language than Latin, Latin must be their language. A complete familiarity with its secrets was therefore their duty as well as their birthright; if such a familiarity escaped them, they must reconquer it.

The results of these conflicting notions will be examined immediately, but it seems necessary first to attempt a conspectus of the whole intellectual period from a more distant viewpoint.

The rediscovery of the remaining books of Aristotle had given a great impetus to philosophical thought, directly as well as indirectly; if the method had not altered, the field of philosophical thought was much widened; physical science was helped out of the earlier stagnation, and problems were faced which had been previously unknown to medieval thinkers. The balance between the *Artes* and philosophy in its wider sense was upset. When it is said that Paris was the real intellectual centre of the epoch, it is implied that philosophy and theology in particular attracted the greatest attention. The early Christian Fathers had been irritated by their own and their contemporaries' partiality for literature and style; the great schoolmen had little of this aversion, because they were indifferent to everything that did not immediately pertain to their subject. When they wrote, they were sincerely anxious to be clear, so as to be easily understood by their readers. Their style cannot be considered debased, for it was the result of their complete familiarity with the κοινὴ διάλεκτος of the schools, a medium which they employed as freely and easily as one deals with one's native language. Among the learned, the language of Rome, if much altered in vocabulary and syntax, had in fact survived, preserving so great a vitality as to become the medium for the expression of thoughts which were alien to the ancients. New words had replaced some words that the Romans had used; words were given a meaning different from the meaning they had formerly expressed; sentences were formed on the pattern provided by vernacular speech rather than classical usage, and the result was a language clear and pliable, excellently suited to the purpose of conveying the thoughts of the schoolmen. But it was no longer the Latin of ancient Rome.

It was partly as the effect of the mass of new ideas which the knowledge of the complete works of Aristotle and of the commentaries transmitted and composed by the Arabs was prompting, that the volume of thought seemed to be breaking through the crust of traditional Latin and to put a new strain on the old language. Christian Latin as well as Christian thought were in open rebellion. Since the twelfth century the purity of the Roman heritage had been menaced by the influx of Greek elements; the philosophical Renaissance was committed to the sacrifice of traditional form to matter.

Then, in the country, let it be once more repeated, where the Latin tradition was strongest and where the memories of Rome were frequently extolled in opposition to foreign power—in the land, in fact, where Rome still spelt civilization and what was not Roman was still considered barbaric—a reaction set in.

There had always been lay schools and lay teachers in Italy side by side with ecclesiastical schools. Otto von Freisingen as well as Wipo had been impressed by the number of laymen who could read and write in Italy; Rudolphus Glaber had commented upon the literary fanaticism of Italians. The study of law, specialized and intensified, offered unexpected opportunities to students who felt no call to enter the Church; city life with its new complexities opened a field of prosperous activity to legally trained students, to good speakers and writers. They might of course have sacrificed form to matter, as many of their contemporaries did, but the traditions of the country in which they lived, and their legal training, were not without effect. At first the masters of *Dictamen* seemed to grope in the dark. That their object was to adorn their style in order to render their words more impressive is obvious; the best means by which such an object could be attained, however, escaped them. They flirted for a considerable time with *cursus*, the use of certain rhythmic clauses in their sentences, and Dante still consistently stuck to this method. But in their search after effect they were driven to the study of classical as well as medieval models. And the Latin authors slowly began to reveal their secret to them.

For some decades they did not dare to depart in public documents and oratory from the current fashion; and yet some among them—lawyers all, if gifted with a keener sensibility for literary craftsmanship than their colleagues—began to play about with poetry. They were still sufficiently medieval to choose Ovid and the elegiac poets as their principal models. Around one or two Paduan masters a small literary group was formed (Rolando da Piazzola, Lovato, Bovetino, Mussato) of men of law who dabbled in poetry, and who were extraordinarily proud of their literary achievement. They were not poets, and they were not scholars in the sense which one would now give to this word. Their knowledge, however, of certain Latin poets was more intimate and at the same time more intelligent than it was in their contemporaries. Above all, they were conscious of striking out on a new path.

It is evident now to everyone that such a turn in literature was not merely a reaction and that it did not stand by itself. New political conditions, city life and wealth, were driving artists also to seek inspiration in classical monuments when building churches and adorning them. There were cities which dared to stand out for their privileges against the popes as well as against the emperors; cities which claimed direct descent from Roman founders and called themselves 'second Romes'. 'Secunda Roma' had been a fairly frequent appellative among cities during the earlier Middle Ages; but then the epithet was employed by poets and had not been adopted by the citizens. Now the citizens seemed to believe in its truth, and felt immensely proud of a name which expressed a deep-rooted conviction. These citizens called themselves Latins.

And thus one passed from the relatively puny efforts of Cermenate and Ferreto to Dante, who openly claimed Virgil as his master, and to Petrarch, who consciously initiated a new method of approach to the ancients. This fashion met in Italy with extraordinary success; it was primarily a reaction against the tyranny of Aristotle and the philosophical methods of the Middle Ages, but, as a result, it brought about a revival of classical studies the influence of which was felt throughout Europe. This rebellion had, however, begun with a finer appreciation of classical form. It was a victory, no matter if a Pyrrhic victory, over the Middle Ages, which had during the later centuries tended to depart from the purely Roman heritage. The Renaissance was on the way.

BIBLIOGRAPHICAL NOTE

H. Bett, *Johannes Scotus Erigena*, Cambridge, 1925.

E. Bishop, *Liturgia historica*, Oxford, 1918.

H. Bresslau, *Die Werke Wipos*, 3rd ed. in SS.RR.GG. in usum scholar., Hannover, 1925.

J. Bryce, *The Holy Roman Empire*, London, 1905.

C. Bursian, *Gesch. d. classischen Philol. in Deutschl.*, München, 1883.

J. B. Bury, *Hist. of the Later Rom. Empire*, London, 1889.

J. Calmette, *La société féodale*, Paris, 1923.

Mélanges offerts à M. E. Chatelain, Paris, Champion, 1910.

D. Comparetti, *Virgil in the Middle Ages* (Engl. trans.), London, 1895.

M. de Wulf, *Hist. of Mediev. Scholasticism* (Engl. trans.), London, 1909.

A. Dresdner, *Kultur u. Sittengesch. der italien. Geistlichkeit im 10. u. 11. Jahrh.*, Breslau, 1890.

E. Dümmler, *Auxilius u. Vulgarius*, Leipzig, 1866.

A. Ebert, *Allgem. Gesch. d. Lit. des Mittelalters im Abendlande*, Leipzig, 1874–87.

Éginhard, *Vie de Charlemagne*, ed. L. Halphen, Paris, 1923.

G. Giesebrecht, *De litterar. studiis apud Italos primis medii aevi saeculis*, Berolini, 1845.

É. Gilson, *La philos. au moyen âge*, Paris, 1922.

Raoul Glaber, *Les cinq livres de ses histoires*, publ. par M. Prou, Paris, 1886.

A. Graf, *Roma nella memoria e nella immaginaz. del M. E.*, Torino, 1882.

G. Gröber, *Grundriss d. latein. Philol.* (2nd ed.)

A. Gwynn, *Roman Education from Cicero to Quintilian*, Oxford, 1926.

T. Haarhoff, *Schools of Gaul*, Oxford, 1920.

C. H. Haskins, *The Renaissance of the Twelfth Century*, Cambridge (U.S.A.), 1927.

B. Hauréau, *Les mélanges poétiques d'Hildebert de Lavardin*, Paris, 1882.

S. Hellmann, *Sedulius Scotus*, in 'Quellen u. Untersuch. z. latein. Philol. des Mittelalt.', München, 1906.

R. Köbner, *Venantius Fortunatus*, in 'Beitr. z. Kulturgesch. d. Mittelalt. u. d. Renaiss.', Hft. 22, Leipzig, 1915.

H. Kuypers, *Studien über Rudolph d. Kahlen*, Goch, 1891.

A. J. Macdonald, *Lanfranc*, Oxford, 1926.

M. Manitius, *Gesch. d. lat. Liter. d. Mittelalters*, München, 1911–24.

W. Meyer, *Gesammelte Abhandl. z. mittellatein. Rythmik*, Berlin, 1905.

E. Norden, *Die antike Kunstprosa*, 2nd ed., Leipzig, 1909.

F. Novati, *L'influsso d. pens. lat. sopra la civiltà ital. d. M. E.*, 2nd ed., Milano, 1899.

F. Novati—A. Monteverdi, *Le origini*, in 'Storia letter. d'It.', Milano, 1900–1925.

A. F. Ozanam, *La civilisation au cinquième siècle*, Paris, 1873.

Patrologiae cursus completus. Patr. Lat., ed. Migne.

Poetae latini aevi Carolini, edd. Dümmler, Traube, Winterfeld, Strecker, in M.G.H.

Poetae latini minores, ed. Lemaire, Paris, 1825.

R. L. Poole, *Illustr. to the Hist. of Mediev. Thought and Learning*, S.P.C.K., 1920.

Rashdall, *The Universities of Europe in the Middle Ages*, London, 1895.

M. Roger, *L'enseignement classique d'Ausone à Alcuin*, Paris, 1905.

U. Ronca, *Cultura mediev. e poesia lat. in Italia nei sec. xi e xii*, Roma, 1892.

Cl. Rutilius Namatianus, éd. crit. par Vesserau, Paris, 1904.

G. Salvioli, *L'istruz. pubbl. in Italia nei sec. viii, ix e x*, Firenze, 1898.

J. E. Sandys, *A Hist. of Classical Scholarship*, 3rd ed., Cambridge, 1921.

F. Schneider, *Rom u. Romgedanke im Mittelalt.*, München, 1926.

H. O. Taylor, *The Classical Heritage of the Middle Ages*, New York, 1901.

H. O. Taylor, *The Medieval Mind*, New York, 1919.

L. Traube, *Vorlesungen u. Abhandlungen*, 3 vols., München, 1909, 1921.

L. Traube, *O Roma nobilis*, in 'Abhandl. d. philos.–philol. Cl. d. Königl. Bayerischen Akademie', Bd. xix (1891).

H. Waddell, *The Wandering Scholars*, London, 1927.

P. V. Winterfeld, *Deutsche Dichter des latein. Mittelalters*, 2nd ed., 1917.

Die Werke Wipos, herausg. von H. Bresslau, 3rd ed., Hannover, 1915.

INDEX

Ademar of Chabannes, 94.
Adriatic Sea, 75.
Aëtius, 29.
Africa, 8, 13, 22, 23, 24, 52, 61, 62.
Africans, 24.
Aix-la-Chapelle, 80, 85, 92.
Alaric, 16, 17, 28, 29, 30.
Albertus Magnus (of Cologne), 105.
Alcuin, 66, 67, 74, 80, 81, 82, 87, 90.
Alps, 79.
Ambrose, St., 32, 36, 42.
Ammianus Marcellinus, 19.
Angilbert (Homerus), 83, 84.
Anglo-Saxons, 61, 62, 63, 64, 65, 67, 68, 76, 78.
Anselm, St., of Aosta, 98, 99, 107.
Anselm of Besate, 94.
Apollinaris, Sidonius, 70, 72.
Apollo, 47.
Appian Way, 39.
Aquinas, St. Thomas, 105, 106, 107.
Arabic, 105, 106.
Arabs, 78, 110.
Arator, 73.
Aristotle, 42, 50, 97, 104, 105, 109, 110.
Arts, The Seven Liberal, 100, 101, 109.
Asturias, 26.
Auctores, 100, 101.
Augustine, St., 32, 36, 42, 47, 55, 66, 69, 87, 90.
Ausonius, 69, 74.
Athens, 45.
Attila, 10, 28, 29, 33.
Avitus, Alcimus, 70.

Bacon, Roger, 105.
Bec, 98.
Bede, 65, 66, 67.
Benedict of Chiusa, 94.
Benedict (St.), 53.

Berengarius of Tours, 99, 100.
Bilbilis, 16.
Biscop, Benedict, 66.
Bobbio, 79, 94.
Boëthius, 46, 48, 49, 50, 51, 52, 60, 73, 87, 91, 100.
Bologna, Univ. of, 94, 107, 108.
Boniface, St., 67, 80.
Bosporus, 29.
Bovetino, 112.
Britain, 8, 13, 65, 68.
Bruno, 92.
Byzantine Emperors. See Emperors, Eastern.

Caesar, 21.
Canterbury, 98.
Capitol, 29.
Carlovingians, 22.
Carlovingian (1) Renaissance. See Renaissance; (2) script, 77, 81.
Cassiodorus, 46, 48, 49, 50, 51, 52, 53, 73.
Catullus, 41.
Cermenate, John of, 113.
Charlemagne, 26, 37, 61, 68, 75, 78, 79, 80, 81, 82, 83, 84, 85, 88, 95.
Charles the Bald, 91.
Chartres, School of, 100, 101.
Cicero, 15, 35, 36, 41, 50, 55, 66, 85, 108.
Claudian, 10, 19, 23, 57.
Clement the Scot, 82.
Clermont-Ferrand, 71.
Clotarius II, 22.
Clovis, 49.
Cluny, 92, 94.
Cologne, 70.
Columban, 80.
Constantine, 29.
Constantinople, 10, 19, 30.
Corbie, 79.
Cordoba, 15.
Cursus, 111.

INDEX

PRINTED IN GREAT BRITAIN AT THE UNIVERSITY PRESS, OXFORD
BY JOHN JOHNSON, PRINTER TO THE UNIVERSITY

154
15·11·29